PONY CLUB MANUAL
No 3: FOR INSTRUCTORS

This is the final volume of the series of three manuals commissioned by the New Zealand Pony Clubs Association, and used also as instruction handbooks by Pony Clubs in Australia, Canada, the United States, and South Africa. *Manuals 1* and *2* cover the Pony Club syllabus for riders, and must be read in conjunction. *Manual No 3* explains how to teach what is contained in the first two books.

Manual No 1, which is for beginning and younger riders, covers basic horse care and knowledge, as well as easy to understand training for D and C Certificates.

These foundations are developed in *Manual No 2*, a more technical book, providing clear and comprehensive instruction for the more advanced Certificates — C+ (13 years+), B (15 years+), A and H (17 years+), and for the competitive older rider.

Manual No 3 is concerned firstly with helping new instructors to understand the Pony Club system and to make a confident start, learning to give clear commands and to handle rides safely in different circumstances.

Secondly, this manual aims to help all instructors to teach riding and horse management at all levels of the Pony Club syllabus, on lines which will ensure enjoyment, variety and maintenance of pupils' interest, as well as improving technical ability.

Instructing has many rewards. Beyond the pleasures and achievements of Pony Club activities there are the ambitions that capture many riders. The examples of double Olympic champion Mark Todd and other outstanding New Zealand event riders, who went through the Pony Club system, present a strong incentive.

Instructors who share in the development of our young riders may well have the satisfaction of following their careers as they gain adult skills and triumphs.

There is no less satisfaction in knowing that you have helped others, on a less exalted plane, to master and enjoy one of the most character-forming sports, which may well lead to lifelong interest and pleasure.

Manual No 3 provides a precise source of reference for teaching and examining, for Pony Club instructors and administrators.

Books by Elaine Knox-Thompson
and Suzanne Dickens

Guide to Riding and Horse Care (Weldon 1977, 1979, 1981,
1984, 1985, 1989)

The Young Horse (Collins 1979, 1985)

Horses and Ponies (Shortland 1989)

Pony Club Manual Number One (1981, 1982, 1984, 1986,
1988, 1990)

Pony Club Manual Number Two (1985, 1988, 1990)

Pony Club Manual Number Three: For Instructors
(1989, 1991)

The three manuals are published by
Ray Richards Publisher
in conjunction with the
New Zealand Pony Clubs Association Inc.

Horse Sense (TVNZ 1982)
Television series by Elaine Knox-Thompson
and Suzanne Dickens

PONY CLUB MANUAL
No 3: For Instructors

by

Elaine Knox-Thompson
BHSI, IIH

and Suzanne Dickens
BHSI, IIH

Drawings by Megan Harvey
Photographs by Suzanne Dickens

Auckland
RAY RICHARDS PUBLISHER

First published 1989
Reprinted 1991

RAY RICHARDS PUBLISHER
49 Aberdeen Road, Auckland 9
in conjunction with
NEW ZEALAND PONY CLUBS ASSOCIATION

ISBN 0-908596-31-6

Designed by Richard King/Edcetera
Typeset by Typocrafters Ltd, Auckland
Printed by Colorcraft Limited

FOREWORD

A valuable series has been completed with the publication of this third Pony Club manual, *Manual No 3 — for Instructors.*

Manual No 1, for D and C levels, has been reprinted six times since its introduction in 1981, and *Manual No 2*, for C+, B, H and A levels, reprinted twice since publication in 1985. The success and popularity of the first two manuals will be reflected in the acknowledgment this third volume will receive.

Manual No 3 has been principally compiled for instructional and training purposes, but it also includes necessary information for parents, riders and officials in Pony Club. Every facet and stage of instruction, from the beginning through to the more advanced levels in Pony Club, is clearly defined, and when used in conjunction with *Manuals 1* and *2*, this book comprehensively details all objectives for the Pony Club instructor.

Elaine Knox-Thompson and Suzanne Dickens, in consultation with other members of the New Zealand Pony Clubs National Instructors' Panel, have written the first two volumes for the environmental conditions of the New Zealand horse and rider, but it is interesting that the universality of their attitudes and experience has resulted in the manuals being increasingly adopted in other countries as well. With the implementation of this third manual the series draws upon the depth of knowledge and resources of the authors' years of experience and establishes an unparalleled reference and learning guide, not only to Pony Club instructors and riders, but to all interested in equestrian sports throughout the world.

As chairperson of the New Zealand Training Committee and on behalf of the members of the Committee of Management and Pony Clubs throughout New Zealand, I would like to compliment the authors on their accomplishments and dedication in producing this remarkable series, and for sharing their knowledge and teaching skills with all who read these three Pony Club manuals.

Ann Roke
Chairperson: Training Committee
New Zealand Pony Clubs Association

ACKNOWLEDGMENTS

When we were commissioned to write these three manuals on behalf of the New Zealand Pony Clubs Association we doubt if anybody, least of all ourselves, thought of it as a ten-year project.

Now, once again, we must thank the Association for their backing and the patience they have shown while awaiting the completion of the task.

To the training committee, and especially their chairperson, Ann Roke, and to the Association president, Roland Matthews, and secretary, Judy Wakeling, our thanks and appreciation for their constant support and assistance.

The encouragement and enthusiasm of our fellow National Instructors, Janey Fisher, Margaret Harris, Kaye Hogan, Anna Monds, Errol O'Brien and Jennifer Stobart (all BHSI) have been a tremendous incentive throughout.

Megan Harvey has again risen magnificently to the challenge of interpreting our often complex and ill-drawn draft plans for the illustrations. Her sense of humour is an essential ingredient of these books.

Pony Club instructors throughout New Zealand and overseas have shown great interest in *Manual No 3*, and many of them have made sound suggestions regarding the contents. Our thanks for the time and trouble that they have taken.

The St John Ambulance Association in Taupo has read, amended and approved the section on safety in Chapter 1. We are most grateful for their suggestions.

Finally, our wonderful publishers. Ray Richards and his family, Barbara and Nicki, must rate as the most patient in the business. Despite the inevitable hold-ups, there has never been any pressure to force things along. We are indeed fortunate to have had their advice and expertise in the production of these books.

Note: For the sake of simplicity, the text of this manual refers to riders, instructors, readers and horses as 'he'.

CONTENTS

9

INTRODUCTION

This is the final volume in the series of three Pony Club manuals. Nos 1 and 2 contain 'what to teach' at all levels, No 3, 'how to teach it', with suggestions for the organisation and administration of all kinds of Pony Club activities.

The instructional system described here, from the individual member and instructor through the branches and clubs to a central organisation, is common, with minor variations, to Pony Clubs throughout the world. The certificates, from D to A and H, are also universal, although the number and content of the actual tests may vary in different countries. Competition is popular everywhere, and all countries hold events of various kinds, from the local gymkhana to the national championships in games, horse trials and other activities.

TO THE PONY CLUB INSTRUCTOR

Pony Club is an instructional youth movement. Without the dedicated work of the many club and branch instructors, it could not function. So when you join the instructional team you are undertaking a vital role in your club.

Please don't be discouraged if this manual appears to be complex. It is necessarily detailed because it sets out to provide for all circumstances and standards of Pony Club instruction and examination. The table of contents makes it easy to locate the subjects you will need at any time.

In common with most other sports, riding has become more technical in recent years. This does put increasing demand on amateur (and professional) instructors and coaches to keep up with developments and explain them in clearly understood and appropriate terms to pupils of different age-groups.

You will find that a well-run Pony Club is one of the friendliest organisations, so do not hesitate, when you feel you need additional help, to seek advice and support from other instructors and club officials. It has been said that at Pony Club you meet the 'nicest possible people in the nicest possible mood', and you will soon realise how true this is.

We hope that the General Notes in Chapter 2 will be helpful to all, in explaining the special requirements of instruction in riding and horse management. Words of command, handling rides and different ways of working them to ensure variety and individual attention are covered in detail. It is suggested that those who are about to attend their first instructors' course should study this chapter beforehand, in conjunction with Chapters 3 and 4, to gain advance information and understanding of what will be taught on the course.

More experienced instructors should find the General Notes useful as a refresher, and perhaps they will offer some inspiration in those blank moments that we all suffer at times.

The aim in Chapters 3 to 6 is to define in more detail the different levels and the approach required for each. They all follow the same pattern: definition of the standard, criteria for instructors, and suggestions for increasing their knowledge and experience.

Then come the instructor's objectives, and ideas for taking rides at the particular level, both on the flat and jumping, and for horse or pony management. Games are a major feature for D and C rides.

There is no intention to be dogmatic in the 'specimen lessons'. They incorporate ideas that have been proved to work and to be enjoyable, and they show how to refer to and use the other two manuals when preparing and giving lessons. These lessons simply provide a starting point. As instructors gain experience and confidence, they will develop their own ideas and methods within the Pony Club system.

Chapter 7 contains guidelines for examiners regarding the conduct of tests, marking system and the format of each test, with suggested timetables. Pony Club relies on its more experienced instructors as examiners, and clubs are responsible for the conduct of examinations.

The rules applying to certificate examination are printed separately, because they are subject to revision from time to time. They will be found in the booklet, *Rules and Guidelines for Pony Club Certificates*, obtainable from the Association secretary.

The facilities and props required for each test are listed in this manual to help clubs to prepare for a smoothly run day, although, of course, prior liaison between examiners and organisers is essential.

Competitions — types, organisation and training — are covered in Chapter 8, treks, camps, hunting, etc., will be found in Chapter 9.

Finally, Chapter 10 contains advice on the facilities that are necessary or desirable for all the foregoing activities, and the management of club grounds and grazing.

Whatever your riding interests, if you like children and ponies you will be sure to find a niche in Pony Club. You are bound to feel diffident at first, but you will be surprised how confidence will grow with study and experience. If you are a competitive rider, it is amazing how much your own ability will improve as a result of your efforts to help others with their problems.

1

THE PONY CLUB
INSTRUCTIONAL SYSTEM

What the system is all about — a child and a pony.

The structure of Pony Club administration is outlined in *Manual No 2*, pages 10–11. It is important for instructors to be familiar with this, particularly as it relates to themselves. To enlarge:

The Training Committee, drawn from members of the Committee of Management, is the body which deals with all matters instructional. It approves the manuals and other literature, as well as videos and films for Pony Club use. Through the National Instructors (who are appointed by the Committee of Management) it arranges courses for senior instructors, examiners' clinics and such other courses and seminars as may be required at national or area level. It decides upon the syllabi for all certificates and the running of examinations. All its recommendations must be ratified by the full Committee of Management.

The National Instructors' Panel consists of experienced, professional instructors with a special interest in Pony Club teaching. A representative attends Committee of Management and Training Committee meetings. The National Instructors are employed by the Association to conduct courses, examinations, etc., as above. Otherwise, they are freelance. Clubs and branches requiring instructors' courses should make direct contact with the National Instructor of their choice.

The National Instructors attend the NZPCA annual conference, where they give lectures or demonstrations, as required. They are always available and willing to help and advise clubs on any instructional problems. The panel meets at regular intervals to discuss teaching methods, compilation and content of the manuals and other instructional matters.

Instructors' record cards are issued and signed on behalf of the New Zealand Pony Clubs Association by the National Instructors. They provide a complete record of all official courses, seminars and clinics attended, and should be taken for signature on all such occasions.

The Area Representative is responsible for the organisation of Association courses and seminars and A and H examinations, and for acting as, or appointing the Technical Delegate at B Certificates in his/her area. Through attendance at Committee of Management meetings, the Area Rep. is in a position to pass on information to and from clubs in the area.

The District Commissioner is the kingpin of the organisation at club level. The DC's main function is to keep the club running smoothly and efficiently and everyone in it happy and interested. The DC should visit branch rallies frequently and get to know officials, instructors, parents and children, to advise and conciliate if difficulties arise. This will, at times, require much tact and wisdom.

The DC also appoints examiners and arranges examinations up to B Certificate within the club.

The Club Chief Instructor should preferably be a capable and experienced instructor, but needs, above all, organising ability, tact and authority. The CCI organises the club's team of instructors (who takes which rides, etc.) and the seasonal programme of instruction at rallies; trains, or arranges the training of B, A and H candidates; puts forward instructors to attend Association courses and clinics and helps the development of new instructors. The CCI should visit each

16

branch as often as possible, and work closely with the club committee and the DC to keep everything running smoothly.

The Branch Head Instructor organises the programme of instruction at branch level, in conjunction with the CCI.

The Club and Branch Instructors are the foundation of the whole edifice.

As mentioned in *Manual No 1*, Pony Club instructors come from all professions and all walks of life — from interested and knowledgeable local horse people, from parents and from associate members. They are invited to instruct by the club or branch.

The following are the qualities to be looked for in a good instructor:

1. A real liking for, and understanding of, young people and horses and ponies. Riding is a partnership between them — the instructor must be able to help them understand one another and to sort out problems fairly and impartially if things go wrong.
2. Enthusiasm, with the desire and the ability to communicate. The ability can usually be developed if the desire is strong enough.
3. Imagination and a sense of humour. The ability to put oneself in the pupil's place and adapt one's approach and vocabulary to different age-groups, without ever 'talking down'. With these qualities instructors will provide varied, interesting and enjoyable lessons.
4. Observation, with the ability to see the picture as a whole and to analyse what is seen.
5. Reliability. Always be punctual, with your lesson prepared.
6. Integrity and sincerity. You can't teach what you don't believe in.
7. Loyalty. To the movement as a whole, its ideals and methods. To the club, branch, and fellow instructors.
8. Self-control, calmness, patience and common sense.
9. Authority and ability to keep order in a genial manner.
10. A good voice, which carries well without shouting. This, too, can be developed with training and practice.

Knowledge, experience and training
Naturally, the more expertise the instructor brings to the task, the better it will be for the pupils, and the more advanced the rides they will be able to take. But no matter how expert the instructor may be as a rider or horse manager, training will be needed in the art of teaching and the Pony Club system. This includes planning of lessons and the many different ways of 'putting it across' to intrigue pupils, stimulate their desire to learn and increase their enjoyment of riding.

Potential instructors should be encouraged to:

17

1. Study the three manuals, which, between them, cover all aspects of the Pony Club's philosophy and teaching.
2. Attend instructors' courses, starting with the D–C course, where the basic methods of instruction are taught.
3. Take every opportunity to watch more experienced instructors at work and study their methods and results.
4. Gain as much experience as possible, and analyse objectively their own successes and failures.

Members can make a start from the age of 14 or 15 by acting as leading files, demonstrators and assistant instructors and by coaching individual candidates for tests which they themselves have passed, but they should not take rides without supervision under the age of 17 years.

ADMINISTRATION AT CLUB AND BRANCH LEVEL

Bearing in mind that Pony Club is an instructional movement, it is essential that at least the Chief and Head Instructors should be closely involved with club and branch administration, particularly with regard to planning the yearly programme of activities and the provision of training facilities. (See Chapter 10.)

PROGRAMME FOR THE YEAR

It is suggested that a small group, consisting perhaps of the District Commissioner, Chief and Head Instructors, should draw up a provisional programme for the coming year. It is important at this stage to make sure that there is a good balance of Pony Club life, and that the programme is designed to cater for the ability, ages and interests of the members. These can vary considerably from year to year. The programme must, of course, be discussed and given final approval by the whole committee.

The programme will include:

Working rallies
A working rally, organised by the branch or club, is one that *all* members are entitled to attend. Some instruction is given or received in Pony Club methods of riding and horse management. Games and other activities are usually included.

This is *the vital* part of the Pony Club system. Everyone should feel equally welcome and valued, and it is largely up to instructors to engender a good club spirit where the older and more experienced willingly assist the new and younger members.

Whenever possible, the Head Instructor or other senior person within the branch should hold a roving commission, moving around between the rides, so that he can assist where necessary; encourage and back up younger instructors; talk to parents, dealing tactfully with any queries that may arise; arrange help with jumps, games, etc.; welcome newcomers; and ensure that everything runs smoothly and to time, with the whole team working harmoniously together.

Duration and frequency of rallies
A day rally, usually starting at 10.30 or 11am and finishing about 3pm, allows time, without undue pressure, for a wide coverage of subjects, including horse management, and for everyone to meet over a picnic lunch. It is suggested that once every three weeks is sufficient for this length of rally.

Morning or afternoon rallies, usually lasting about three hours, should not consist entirely of riding, but should include some horse management and a short break, off ponies, for refreshments and a social period at halftime, otherwise they can become too intensive. These could be held every two or three weeks.

Evening rallies can be held during daylight saving. Probably lasting about two hours, these will not allow time to cover everything, so the series must be carefully planned to give a good balance. Certainly avoids shows and competitions and leaves everybody free at weekends. Could be held weekly.

When deciding what is best for your club, consider: the number of instructors available, and the instructor/pupil ratio; whether the instructors are competitive riders; and where the club members ride, whether mainly on the club grounds or elsewhere. In the former case, supervision will have to be provided, and more frequent rallies may be desirable.

Weekly rallies, held at weekends, put great strain on the instructors, most of whom either ride and wish to compete themselves, or have other interests and commitments. But a roster system, often used in these cases, means that it is almost impossible to assess an individual rider's progress, even if continuity is maintained.

Generally speaking, longer rallies held less frequently are recommended, but clubs may find that a mixture of the different types could be utilised during the year.

Competitions
Club and branch gymkhanas and/or games days, horse trials at various levels, area trials. Possibly qualifying rounds for dressage

championships, other inter-club or area competitions.

Competitions must not be allowed to predominate to the virtual exclusion of everything else. This discourages the less competitive members, and leads others to enter events for which they have had insufficient preparation, with consequent frustration all round. More time for training at rallies, with a higher standard of performance at fewer competitions, is greatly to be preferred.

Test days
Any time for D Certificate, preferably twice a year for C, once or twice for C+ and B.

Other activities
Treks, camps and other more relaxed activities are invaluable for teaching practical horsemanship and behaviour when riding with others, as well as care and consideration of the pony or horse.

Items that might well be included in the programme are: organised outings to championships, three-day events, sales, saddlers and other places and events of interest to members at various stages; visiting speakers; and, of course, social activities.

When the programme is finalised and the number and duration of rallies known, detailed programmes for each ride can be compiled. They could be outlined by the Chief and Head Instructors in consultation and finalised after full discussion at an instructors' meeting, generally covering six rallies at a time. Towards the end of the period, a review of progress should be made, and a plan considered for the next six rallies.

Forward planning is necessary to ensure the syllabus is covered in a methodical way, with variety and continuity of instruction. While it is desirable that the same instructor should take a ride throughout the season to establish a rapport with the members and get to know their ponies and their problems, a formal plan will allow some other instructor to take over if necessary and maintain continuity.

Members will be more likely to attend regularly if they recognise a thread of logic running through the lessons and realise that there will be gaps in their knowledge if they miss rallies.

THE SYLLABUS OF INSTRUCTION

This syllabus covers all instruction at Pony Club from Pre-D level up to A and H Certificates. It is divided in this way for convenience — it is not intended that the division should put undue emphasis on the taking of examinations. If this system is properly used, with sufficient revision at each stage, work required for certificates should be covered in the normal course of events at rallies, and no special coaching should be needed up to C+.

For the member starting as a beginner at the age of about eight, each stage will take approximately one season. However, new members join at all ages and stages of ability, so consideration as to where to fit them in must be given.

Whatever happens, everybody must cover the whole syllabus *at their own pace*. Some will naturally progress faster than others, particularly in jumping or other aspects that appeal to them, but it must always be borne in mind that our aim is to produce all-round horsemen and women, not specialists in any one branch of riding.

Members' record cards, available from the Association secretary for each certificate, set out the syllabus, with space for the date and the instructor's signature when each subject has been taught and understood. This ensures that the syllabus is covered without any gaps, and also acts as an incentive to the member to get the card filled up. The card should be completed before sitting the appropriate test.

Each of the syllabus stages should be taught consecutively.

D CERTIFICATE

There is one stage towards D Certificate:

STAGE PRE-D

Riding
Mount and dismount.
Know the correct position and how to hold the reins.
Ride without a leading rein.
Rising trot.
Simple aids for transitions and turns.
Exercises and reasons for doing them.
Do's and don'ts when riding on the road.
Games.
Start: canter, walk/trot over scattered poles, walk on long rein.
    (Last three not in D Certificate.)

Pony care and other instruction
Approach and handle a pony, give a titbit.
Catch pony and put on halter, turn out into paddock.
Tie pony up correctly.

Lead in hand at walk.
Brush pony over.
Points of the pony.
Parts of the saddle and bridle.
Know name of own instructor, branch and club.
Check record cards and revise before sitting D.
Recommended minimum age for D Certificate, 8 or 9 years.

C CERTIFICATE

There are three stages towards C Certificate:

STAGE PRE-C1

Riding
Turnout of pony and rider.
Mount and dismount on either side.
Reasons for maintaining the correct position.
Improving position — all paces.
Rising trot, sitting trot, trot without stirrups, holding saddle.
Exercises at halt and walk.
Diagonals.
Riding with reins in one hand.
Holding and use of whip.
Alter stirrups, adjust girth when mounted.
Understand the meaning of the word 'aids'.
Natural and artificial aids.
20m circles, walk and trot.
Canter on named leg on circle or corner.
Paces, rhythm and regularity.
Walk on long rein.
Ride up and down slopes, walk and trot.
Jumping position.
Trotting poles.
Jump very small fences at trot.
Short course small fences, correct track, at trot/canter.
Riding on road — correct side, use of hand signals.
Games, gymkhanas.

Pony care and other instruction
Requirements of a pony at grass.
Care of pony with the change of seasons.
Feeding hay.

Safety factors when handling ponies.
Lead in hand at walk and trot.
Reasons for grooming.
Use and care of grooming tools.
Picking up and picking out feet.
Care of the mane and tail.
Know when the pony needs shoeing.
Signs of good and bad health.
When to ask advice.
Saddle and bridle — fitting of own pony's tack.
Name and action of own pony's bit.
Put on and take off a cover.
Cleaning tack.
Points of the pony, colours and markings.
Description and measurement of ponies.
Know name of branch Head Instructor.

STAGE PRE-C2

Riding
Revise Stage Pre-C1.
Further improvement in position, clearer application of aids with
    better co-ordination.
Short trots without stirrups.
Further work on circles, all paces.
More accurate transitions, including canter.
Use of whip to reinforce leg.
Meaning of free forward movement and of pony accepting the bit.
Halt and salute.
Junior riding test.
Trot on a long rein.
Further hill work.
Open and shut a gate, dismounted and mounted.
Improve jumping position.
Contact over trotting poles and jumps.
Jump at trot and canter.
Simple, two-stride doubles.
Further courses. Insist on rhythm, correct bend and track before
    increasing height.
Jumping without reins.
Riding on the road. Safety precautions when leading or riding a
    pony out on to a road, road signs, overtaking stationary vehicles,
    dealing with a pony shying on the road.

Behaviour when riding out and about, alone or in company.
Games, gymkhanas/shows.

Pony care and other instruction
Revise Stage Pre-C1.
Choosing and daily care of a paddock.
Elementary watering and feeding.
Feeding pellets and chaff.
Better standard of grooming — use of body brush in summer.
The pony's foot. Types of shoes.
Recognise high clench, shoe on corn place, excessive rasping.
Dosing for worms — why, how and when.
Rasping of teeth — why needed.
Coughs, colds, colic.
Isolation.
Sunburn, bit injuries, girth and saddle galls, cover rubs.
First-aid kit.
Know name of District Commissioner.

STAGE PRE-C3

Riding
Revise Stage Pre-C2.
Confirm position and application of aids.
Pony accepting the bit, with regularity and some activity.
Preliminary dressage test, Prix Caprilli.
Ride up and down hill, all paces.
Ride through water.
Ride smoothly over show jumps, including one- or two-stride
    doubles, showing steady position and contact.
Jump small ditches.
Jump small fences on slopes.
Introductory Pony Club horse trials.
Riding on the road. Riding in traffic. Riding at dusk or in poor
    visibility. Know the Road Code.
Games.

Pony care and other instruction
Revise Stage Pre-C2.
Feeding and exercise.
Recognition of feedstuffs.
Care and cleaning of covers.
Loading and unloading.

Treating wounds.

Anti-tetanus inoculation.

Treating: kicks and bruises; lice, ticks, ringworm; laminitis and grass staggers.

General care of a sick or injured pony.

Names and locations of other local Pony Club branches.

Check record cards and revise before sitting C Certificate.

Recommended minimum age for C Certificate, 11 or 12 years.

Maximum height of fences for C Certificate, 60cm (2ft).

C+ and B CERTIFICATES

There are two stages towards C+, and a further two stages to B:

STAGE PRE-B1

Riding

Revise C work.

Position becoming deeper and steadier.

Exercises, halt, walk, trot.

Apply aids accurately.

Footfalls at all paces.

Work on 'feel' at walk, diagonals, leading leg, etc.

Understand the terms balance, straightness, rhythm, tempo, impulsion.

Pony should accept all aids and be showing improved balance.

Improve 20m circles in canter.

15m circles in walk and trot.

Loop.

Quarter-turn on forehand.

Begin lengthening in trot.

Canter on long rein.

Ride up and down steep hills.

Judgment of speed and distance — walk and trot.

Strong canter in the open, pull up smoothly.

Reasons for jumping position — effects of faults.

Ride simple gymnastic exercises and combinations. Be aware of good distances for own pony.

Jump small, varied cross-country fences, including banks, drops, ditches and water.

Walk, and ride, a show-jumping course.

Pre-training horse trials.

Planning a training programme.

Pony management
Revise C work.
Daily care of pony and paddock.
Recognise poisonous plants.
Principles of watering, feeding and exercise.
Recognise oats, barley, bran. Know their uses.
Make a bran mash.
Handle pony safely and efficiently. Lead in and out of a yard.
Groom a pony effectively.
Care of pony after show, hunting or other long day.
Names and uses of different clips.
Names of parts of the foot and shoe.
Names and uses of farrier's tools.
Putting on travel boots and bandages, including tail bandage.
When to call the vet and what to have on hand when he comes.
Bathing and dressing wounds.
Hosing for treatment of wounds, sprains, etc.
Internal parasites — types.
Running up in hand for lameness or action.
Fitting tack.
Care and cleaning of equipment.

STAGE PRE-B2

Riding
Revise Stage Pre-B1.
Be aware of faults in position and how to improve.
Improve co-ordination of aids.
Be able to discuss pony's balance and way of going.
10m circles in walk.
Three-loop serpentine, walk and trot.
Half-turn on forehand.
Lengthened strides in trot.
Change of leg through trot.
Concept of riding from inside leg to outside hand.
Meaning of 'on the bit'.
Judgment of speed and distance — canter, cross-country pace.
Gallop.
Confirm jumping position and contact.
Dealing with own pony's jumping problems.
Walk, and ride, cross-country course.
Training level Pony Club horse trials.

Pony management
Revise Stage Pre-B1.
Recognise good and bad hay.
Recognition and uses of listed feedstuffs.
Bringing up after a spell.
Principles of getting pony fit.
How to prepare pony for clipping.
Discuss own pony's shoeing.
Poulticing, tubbing, fomenting.
Discuss own pony's worming programme.
Bits in everyday use.
Check record cards and revise before sitting C+.
Minimum age for C+ Certificate, 13 years.
Maximum height of fences, 75cm (2ft 6in).

STAGE PRE-B3

Riding
Revise C+ work.
Work on improving depth and independence of position.
Apply aids accurately and sympathetically.
Half-halt.
Working trot and canter.
Difference between 'accepting' and 'on' the bit.
Riding in position.
10m circles in trot.
Decrease and increase of circle.
Start demi-pirouette, lengthening in canter.
Ride with two pairs of reins on snaffle.
Knowledge of speed and distance.
Show good control in gallop.
Change horses on the flat.
Work on strengthening jumping position over all types of fences.
Use of trotting poles to adjust horse's stride.
Building schooling fences. Combination distances.

Horse management and other instruction
Revise C+ work.
Paddock maintenance.
Understand principles of conditioning and getting fit. Signs of
   fitness. Roughing off.
Holding a horse for treatment, shoeing, etc.
Quartering and strapping. Make and use a wisp.

Cooling down after fast work.
Pulling and plaiting the mane.
Trimming heels with scissors and comb.
Know the five stages of shoeing.
Prepare horse for travel.
Knowledge of loading/unloading, care during a journey.
Points to check in a loose box, use of stable tools.
Lead horse in and out of a loose box.
Know normal temperature, pulse and respiration. Take respiration.
Detection of heat, pain and swelling.
Reporting horse's symptoms to the vet.
Conformation — balance and proportion, terms in common use.
Working boots and bandages.
Action of the three basic types of bits.
Know the objects of the Pony Club.
Responsibilities of a Pony Club member.

STAGE PRE-B4

Riding
Revise Stage Pre-B3.
Further work to establish position.
Understand the importance of balance, straightness, rhythm,
    tempo, impulsion.
Circle exercises.
Canter from walk.
Demi-pirouette.
Ride with a double bridle.
Ride and jump each other's horses, discuss their way of going.
Show a balanced position and effective contact over all types of
    fences. Jump show and cross-country courses.
Use of poles and exercises to improve a horse's jumping.
Common causes of jumping faults.

Horse management and other instruction
Revise Stage Pre-B3.
Vitamin and mineral additives.
Plaiting the tail.
Recognise good and bad shoeing.
Types of bedding — management of each type.
Stable routine over a limited period.
What to look for, morning and evening.
Dealing with 'breaking out' and with a 'cast' horse.

Care of the horse away from home.
Some knowledge of 'tying-up', and of sprains and splints.
Good and bad points of conformation and action.
Names and recognition of teeth.
Care, cleaning and storage of equipment.
Inspection of saddlery for soundness.
Some knowledge of the organisation of the NZPCA.
Name of the National President.
Check record cards and revise before being assessed for B
    Certificate. If possible, attend an examination as a spectator.
Minimum age for B Certificate, 15 years.
Maximum height of fences, 90 cm (3ft).

A and H CERTIFICATES

There are two stages towards A and H Certificates:

STAGE PRE-A1

Riding
Revise B work.
Further work on position, including on lunge, if possible.
Use of seat and weight aids.
Improvement in the quality of the horse's paces.
Medium paces.
Demi-pirouette.
Simple change of leg.
Principles of lateral work.
Leg yielding.
Shoulder-in.
Pace work.
Ride and jump as many different horses as possible. Discuss their
    problems and how they could be improved.
Jumping position becoming more adaptable and polished, with
    accurate contact and stride control.
Greater understanding of the principles of gymnastic jumping.
Gain further experience in dressage, horse trials and other
    competitions.

Horse management and other instruction (A and H Certificates)
Revise B work.
Pasture management.
Elementary knowledge of the horse's digestive system and
    nutritional requirements.

Feeding and conditioning programmes.
Washing a horse's sheath.
Pulling a tail.
Use and care of a clipping machine.
Some knowledge of the anatomy of the horse's foot.
Use of screw-in studs.
Be able to remove a shoe.
Elementary knowledge of stable construction.
Fire precautions in stables.
Stable routine.
Construction and use of yards.
Travelling horses, inspection of float, loading difficult horses.
Take a horse's pulse and temperature.
Sick nursing.
Symptoms of dehydration.
Internal parasites — use of anthelmintics.
Detection of lameness and its possible cause.
Foot ailments, sprains, sore shins, interfering.
Basic knowledge of the horse's structure and anatomy.
Examining the teeth for sharp edges and wolf teeth.
Different types of saddles. Recognise a broken tree.
Principles of bitting and uses of different bits.
Uses of various covers, rugs and sheets.
Basic principles of training the young horse.
Tack up and lunge a horse — reasons for lunging.
Ride and lead two compatible horses.
Assist a rider to mount. Give a leg up.
The Pony Club — its formation, objects and organisation.
Other organisations connected with horses and ponies.
Horse and pony breeds.

STAGE PRE-A2

Riding
Revise Stage Pre-A1.
Continue to work on improving position.
Apply all the aids unobtrusively and effectively.
Counter canter.
Rein back.
Shoulder-in and other lateral movements.
Continue to ride, jump and assess horses at all stages of training.
Discuss schooling plans.

Ride with confidence and determination over all types of fences, showing a strong, correct and adaptable position.

Build suitable fences, exercises and courses to encourage good style in a horse's jumping.

Horse management and other instruction (A and H Certificates)
Revise Stage Pre-A1.
Management of a number of horses at grass. Pasture assessment.
Assessment of quality of feedstuffs.
Purchase and storage of forage and bedding.
Use of electrolytes.
Principles of interval training.
Handling difficult horses — use of a twitch.
Clipping a horse, hogging a mane.
Changes in the foot resulting from neglect, poor shoeing or disease.
Remedial shoeing (e.g., feather-edged shoes, grass tips, soles).
Siting and building a muck heap.
Vices and bad habits of stabled horses.
Respiratory ailments.
Azoturia. Tetanus.
Strangles, cough epidemics, etc.
Seats of lameness — bony and bursal enlargements.
Conformation — how it affects soundness and usefulness.
Ageing by the teeth.
Buying a horse.
Care, maintenance and fitting of all types of equipment.
Protective clothing for the horse.
Organisation of a tack room.
Outline of the education of a young horse.
Approved Pony Club training methods.
Knowledge of running of own branch/club.
Attend basic instructors' course. (Optional.)
Assist with coaching/instruction/administration.
Attend A and/or H examinations as a spectator (or groom for H).
Revise before A/H Certificate.
Be assessed for A Certificate.
Maximum height of fences for A Certificate, 1.15m (3ft 9in).
H Certificate candidates must have a very thorough and practical knowledge of all the horse management sections of the syllabus.
Minimum age for A and H Certificates, 17 years.

SAFETY FACTORS

When dealing with such unpredictable elements as children and ponies, occasional falls and accidents are bound to occur. To keep these to a minimum, certain precautions and rules are necessary. They should be as few and as unobtrusive as possible, but must be strictly observed. The following are suggested:

1. Every member's address and telephone number should be readily available at rallies.
2. Whenever possible the clubroom should be on the telephone.
3. First-aid boxes for riders and horses should always be available and kept well stocked.
4. Instructors must be aware of any disabilities of members — e.g., diabetes, asthma, old injuries.
5. It is most desirable that at least one person at a rally (not necessarily an instructor) should have a first-aid certificate. Instructors should be urged to study first aid. A talk, or even a short course, might be arranged with a qualified person, who also has a knowledge of riding and Pony Club.
6. Pony Club approved headgear and safe footwear *must* be worn by all riders, whether members or not, whenever they are riding on club grounds.

Back and body protectors are available for cross-country and other strenuous jumping, and older members should be informed of this, although their use is not compulsory.

Supportive underwear for both girls and boys can do much to prevent injury and ensure comfort when riding. Girls develop greatly between the ages of about 12 and 15. The use of a sports bra will protect the breast muscles, as well as helping the rider to maintain a steadier position.

Boys often suffer much discomfort from saddles with a high or exaggeratedly narrow pommel. A lower pommel, ideally with a cut back head, and a broader, flatter seat will help. Boys should be advised to wear an athletic support — obtainable from sportswear shops or chemists.

7. Road gates must never be left open.
8. No jumping should be allowed on Pony Club grounds without adult supervision.
9. Ponies may be ridden at walk only in the vicinity of the clubroom and in other 'heavy traffic' areas. Indiscriminate galloping about should be forbidden everywhere.
10. All rides start with inspection. It must be clearly understood that

unsafe gear is to be replaced or made safe before the rider may take part in any activity.

11. Instructors must be aware of young or difficult ponies. Clubs have the right to debar ponies that are dangerous to other members or to their own riders, either when ridden or in grazing. Stallions and rigs, if well behaved, may be ridden but not grazed at Pony Club. When tied up they should be kept apart from other horses.

12. Safety factors in handling ponies (*Manual No 1*, page 141, and *Manual No 2*, page 13) must be taught and observed at all times at Pony Club. Possible consequences of dangerous actions should always be pointed out.

13. Proper tying-up facilities should be provided and used, with ponies correctly tied up at all times.

14. Great attention must be paid to safety factors when organising grazing (see page 210).

ACCIDENTS

Riders should be told early on that everybody falls off sometimes — it's no big deal. Explain that it is important to curl up and relax as much as possible. Don't throw out an arm to break your fall or try to hang on to the pony.

In the event of a fall, if there is no serious injury (maybe a slight bump, tears and fright), sympathise, reassure, but make as little fuss as possible. Try to get the child up on the pony again quickly. If jumping, the rider should go back to something small and easy to restore confidence.

If there is injury, keep calm, halt the ride, get help either to attend to the casualty or to keep the ride occupied. Don't let people crowd round. Reassure the casualty, keeping them quiet and still, at least until the extent of the injury has been determined.

If there is any possibility of concussion, the child must not be allowed to ride again that day, and their parents should be informed.

Apart from falls when riding, the principal causes of accidents around horses are incorrect or careless tying-up, kicks, being trodden on or knocked over by a pony, occasionally bites. The above measures, applied consistently with firmness and common sense, should do everything possible to guard against such incidents.

Log-book. It is strongly recommended that a log-book be kept by clubs/branches, giving details of accidents involving injury or damage to property. This record may be useful for accident compensation or insurance purposes.

2
GENERAL NOTES
FOR INSTRUCTORS

Pony Club instructors in conference. People of all ages, from all walks of life.

All instruction at Pony Club is based on *Manuals 1* and *2*.

Good instruction should be constructive and interesting, stimulating the desire to learn. For younger riders, short periods of tuition must be reinforced by games and 'fun' activities. Safety, enjoyment and some degree of achievement are vital for all.

The Pony Club instructor is the link between knowledge and the member. Good presentation creates confidence and ensures that this knowledge is put across to the best effect.

Always be (or try to be!):

Well turned out. If mounted, or intending to ride at any stage, turnout should at least equal that expected from the class, i.e., hard hat, tidy hair, polished boots, neat shirt and tie or sweater, whip, preferably gloves.

If unmounted, jodhpurs or neat trousers are in order, the latter certainly for horse-management lessons. Do not wear shorts, suntops, fancy blouses or jewellery. Dresses are generally unsuitable.

Always wear solid, low-heeled boots or shoes, not sandals, thongs, trainers or gumboots.

A good example. Posture is important. Avoid slouching with hands in pockets. When mounted, be sure to sit correctly at all times, not only when demonstrating. *Never* smoke or swear when teaching.

Audible. Face the ride, stand upwind, and look up. Work on voice production. Most women need initially to lower the pitch and steady the pace, but variations in volume, pitch, tone and pace are essential to avoid monotony. Breathe deeply and regularly. No breath, no voice!

Try to learn to throw your voice, especially when giving commands. If you have difficulty in making yourself heard or are worried about voice production, a few lessons from an expert on the subject could be invaluable.

A loud-hailer is a useful aid in windy conditions, or when teaching jumping, particularly cross-country. When using a loud-hailer or a microphone, keep your voice down and let the machine do the work.

Positive. Say 'do' rather than 'don't'. For example, 'Look up' is better than 'Don't look down'.

Encouraging of effort or the slightest improvement, though saving your maximum praise for total achievement. Be sure to notice and remark upon any individual improvement since the last rally.

If strong censure is necessary, don't dwell on it, and find something to praise as soon as possible.

Approachable. Get to know each member of your ride and their ponies individually. Members (and parents and other instructors) should feel they can talk to you and discuss any problems freely.

Vigilant. Watch your ride as a whole and be quick to prevent dangerous situations from developing, e.g., children riding up too close behind other ponies. Check that Pony Club methods and principles are being followed at all times, especially in such basic matters as mounting, altering stirrups and tying-up.

Punctual. Arrive early, so that you can have all requirements set up beforehand and be ready to start on time.

Adaptable. It may not always be possible to take the ride exactly as you planned. Weather, the state of the ground, a delay at some point, the behaviour or fitness of the ponies, can all necessitate last-minute changes.

Instructing mounted or unmounted?

If you intend to instruct mounted, be sure that:

1. Your horse is suitable. His turnout, including tack and shoeing, must be of a high standard. He must be sufficiently well schooled to demonstrate the work you are teaching, stand quietly for long periods without distracting your attention from the ride, and be absolutely foolproof with other horses. A good demonstration horse is an invaluable asset.

2. Your own position and ability will be a good example to the ride. Younger children, in particular, imitate what they see, and everyone will be quick to notice if what you teach varies greatly from what you do.

Given the above essentials, the advantages of being mounted are:

1. You can give your own demonstrations, not only of the correct way, but also of faults as they occur.

2. You can ride beside a pupil and show him exactly what he is doing wrong, and what you want him to do.

3. You are more mobile when working a ride in a large area or moving from place to place. Obviously, you must be mounted if you are going to take the ride out for a hack.

4. For B and A rides, if your horse is really well trained and has a good temperament, you might occasionally allow suitable members to ride him in order to get the feel of a horse going correctly in more advanced work.

Bringing a horse to a rally involves more work for the instructor in its preparation and transport, but there is no doubt that members enjoy seeing their instructors mounted, at least sometimes, and getting to know their horses.

Instructing unmounted is generally better with very junior rides. The closer contact makes control easier and gives confidence to the pupils. Altering tack or jumps is far more difficult for a mounted instructor. Inclement weather can also be a problem.

TEACHING

Teaching is communication. For a physical skill such as riding it consists of explanation, demonstration and assessment on the part of the instructor, and understanding, practice, effort and improvement on the part of the pupil.

Explanation must be simple, clear and concise, always geared to the age-group, ability and experience of the class.

Explanation can create or kill interest.

Demonstration is essential, especially when teaching new movements or subjects, to show what is required and how to achieve it.

If you are unmounted, demonstrate by:

1. Using an older member or junior instructor. In this case, be sure to brief your assistant beforehand so that he can prepare himself and his horse.

2. Using a member of the ride, but not the same person every time (this smacks of favouritism and may give the chosen one inflated ideas). Use different people to show different things.

Some instructors find it difficult to explain and demonstrate at the same time, and windy conditions can make it almost impossible for anyone. Using another person to demonstrate can have the advantages of enabling you to explain what is going on as it happens, to answer questions and maintain the attention of the ride.

3. Borrowing a pony from the ride. Be sure to choose a co-operative pony with a suitable saddle. If the stirrups are too small, either cross them and ride without, or use your own.

4. Showing what is wanted on foot — e.g., shape of circles, footfalls. It is surprising how much can be demonstrated in this way.

Any demonstration, unless deliberately showing faults, must be correct. If something does go wrong, never try to gloss it over. Point out the fault and show the proper way. The better the preparation beforehand, the less likely it is that this situation will arise.

Everything you do at Pony Club is a form of demonstration.

Assessment gauges the level of success. Begin by looking at the picture as a whole, at the balance and harmony between pony and rider. Know just what you expect at each level (see Chapters 3 to 6). Even if you take only junior rides, a knowledge of what lies ahead will help you to keep your teaching in perspective.

An instructor must have, or develop, a good 'eye' so that he can:

1. Get to the root cause of faults and problems quickly.

2. Recognise and encourage the slightest improvement, *while it is actually occurring*, and confirm achievement immediately.

This prompt recognition of progress will fire the rider's enthusiasm and help him to appreciate the 'feel' of what he is trying to do.

The ability to assess is essential for progressive teaching.

GIVING A LESSON

A lesson consists of eight parts:

1. Preparation. Decide exactly what you are going to teach. Do not try to cover too much in one lesson. It is always better to teach a little well.

Know your subject. Read it up in the appropriate manual and, if applicable, work on it with your own horse. Try to anticipate any questions that might be asked. If in doubt, discuss it with more senior instructors.

Write down the main points in a logical sequence. Then condense your notes into headings which can be written on a card for quick reference. Decide what equipment you will need — school, jumps, flags, markers, etc.

2. Explanation. The subject of the lesson, its objects, and the reasons for doing it.

3. Demonstration. Clear, uncluttered and correct. Explanation continues simultaneously, pointing out the method, aids and how it should look and feel. Do not show faults at this stage.

4. Invite questions.

5. Practice. All together if possible, or at least in sections, so that riders can practice while it is fresh in their minds. Watch carefully, encourage and assist, and note faults that should be demonstrated.

6. Demonstration of faults. Demonstrate only those faults which have actually occurred. Draw attention to the effects of poor position or unclear aids. Always finish with the correct method.

7. Further practice. Look for and encourage improvement, and help every individual to achieve at least some degree of success.

8. Prove the lesson. Question the ride to ensure that the lesson has been absorbed and understood. Advise on practice at home.

Note that explanation and demonstration together should never occupy more than a quarter of the lesson time. The essential part is practice, with constructive comment and encouragement by the instructor.

A 'lesson of the day' on these lines will form a major part of most periods of riding or jumping instruction at rallies. See page 37.

TAKING RIDES ON THE FLAT

This section includes suggestions on where to work rides — in the open, in the school; controlling a ride — words of command; what to work on — exercises, movements and how they should be carried out; and work in rides, double ride, musical and activity rides.

In the open
1. On a large circle. Generally about 30 to 40m in diameter, depending on the number in the ride, and using markers if required for junior rides.

The ride usually works in 'open order', evenly spaced round the circle. A rider getting too close to the person in front should look round for a space and, without altering the pace, circle *inwards* to fit into it. If riders are alert, this should not often be necessary, as the track can be adjusted in or out to gain or lose distance.

The advantages of this system are that riders learn to look where they are going and think for themselves, but don't have to worry about keeping a set spacing. Horses can work at their own best pace without having to conform exactly to the leader. This is unavoidable in the set track of the school, unless the ride is small enough to work independently. Horses are more attentive to their riders when working farther apart.

The circle is one of the best possible suppling exercises. If horses do not bend correctly on the large circle, they certainly will not achieve good corners in the school.

This work is very useful for establishing free forward movement, rhythm and bend before going into the school.

The instructor should stand still, on the upwind side of the circle rather than in the centre, either just inside or outside the track. You can then speak to each rider individually as they approach and pass close to you. If outside, you can see the position of the rider's outside leg, as well as the straightness of the rider and the bend of the horse, particularly as they go away from you.

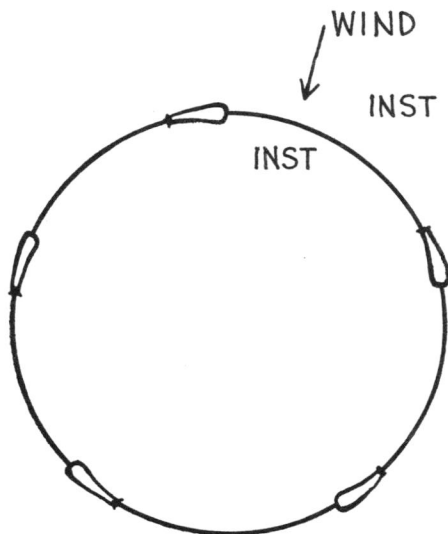

A ride working in open order on a large circle.

There must always be a clearly stated objective — without it, going round in circles soon becomes extremely boring for all concerned.

With the ride closed up to a suitable distance, the following school exercises may be carried out on the large circle: trot/canter from front to rear of the ride (page 50), passing the ride on the inside (page 51) and circling from front to rear (page 52).

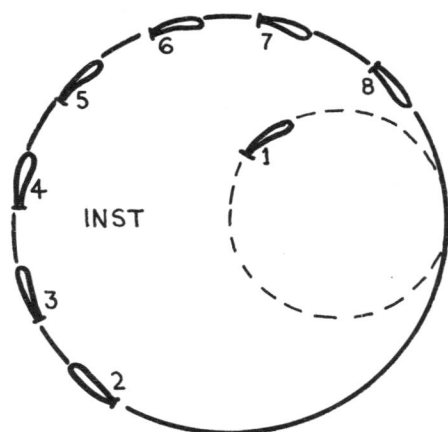

The exercise trot/canter from front to rear of the ride, with a circle inwards. The ride is closed up to one length apart, at walk.

Another useful exercise is to trot/canter from front to rear, with a circle inwards, size to suit the ability of each pony, about three-quarters of the way round the big circle.

2. Working independently, within a defined area. May be:

(a) Commanded by the instructor as to pace and requirements.

(b) Following a pre-stated outline from the instructor — e.g., general work-in, circles, turn on the forehand, lengthening of stride. Best with small numbers, so that the instructor can move around and watch and comment on one or two at a time. When riders have achieved to the best of their ability, they should walk on a long rein, keeping out of the way until all are finished.

(c) Completely freelance. Most suitable for post-C+ rides. Enables riders to concentrate on their own problems and work at their own pace, and allows for consultation with the instructor.

This independent work is essential training for B and A Certificate candidates.

In the school
Arena usually 40 by 20m. 60 by 20m may be used for larger or more

advanced rides. 60 by 30m may be needed for double or formation rides. For permanent arenas, see page 207.

The school may be used by:

1. Juniors — as a 'play-pen', a confined area where they can learn to 'start, stop and steer' and generally control their ponies before venturing into wider spaces.

2. D and C rides. See *Manual No 1*, pages 74–76. The main point is the accuracy of control that develops through the various group and individual exercises. These rides should not be worked for long periods in a school.

3. Intermediate and senior rides, C+, B and A. To develop further precision in movements and transitions. Must still be balanced by work in the open on paces and maintenance of forward movement.

4. Riders preparing for dressage tests. Work in a school is a necessity. See *Manual No 1*, page 103. Members should be strongly urged to put up a school at home, but should still practise in one at Pony Club, under the supervision of their instructor.

Terms and expressions used in the school are listed in *Manual No 1*, page 73. All instructors should make themselves familiar with these, and ensure that their pupils know and understand them, and that they know their left from their right.

School work/exercises/ movements may be performed:

1. In single file. The instructor must insist that everyone rides accurately to the markers and through the corners to the best of their ability, and that the required distance is maintained — in itself, an excellent discipline in control of the pony.

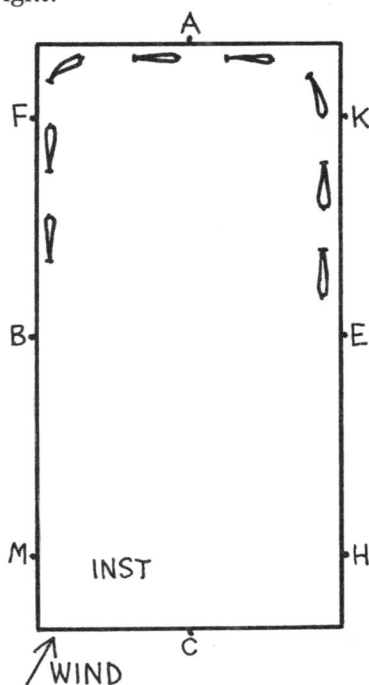

A ride working in the school. They are one length apart — the best distance for most school exercises. A good place for the instructor to stand.

Work in single file is useful when working in, working on riders' positions or learning the shape of new movements, such as circles or serpentines. At the same time, too much of this can quickly become boring, with ponies automatically following the one in front.

Choice of leader is important — choose someone who can establish steady, regular paces, and, preferably, who knows what is required.

Always put bigger horses towards the front of the ride, smaller ones to the rear, where they may take short cuts when necessary to maintain their distance.

Be sure to speak to every member of the ride — a common fault is to address all remarks to the first one or two and forget the others.
2. In succession — for example, trotting, cantering or circling from front to rear of the ride. Excellent for enabling the instructor to give individual attention to each member of the ride while keeping all on the move. *Everybody* must receive constructive comment during their turn.
3. In 'rides' or sections, which keeps everyone, including the instructor, on their toes. As you gain confidence and experience in the timing of commands, you should be able to make brief individual comments.
4. A double ride, generally working on opposite reins.
5. Dividing the ride into two or more sections, one working, the others watching and commenting. Gives more space when working on new or complicated movements, encourages the watchers to learn by observation and allows for different levels of ability within the ride.

Try to include at least two of these methods in every period to ensure variety and individual attention. How this is done depends on the size and standard of the ride, the movements to be practised and the time available.

Individual work for D and C rides usually takes the form of exercises in succession. Otherwise, with a ride of ten, even five minutes work for each person will result in 45 minutes' watching.

With smaller, more advanced rides, individual work, with discussion involving the whole group, is invaluable.

Rules for independent work in the school
1. Riders must be alert and look where they are going.
2. Riders meeting on opposite reins in the school pass left hand to left hand.
3. When walking, use the inside track.
4. Never halt in the track.

5. Never overtake another rider, except one walking on the inside track. Turn or circle away in plenty of time.

6. Riders practising lateral or other advanced movements have right of way, and others must give way to them.

7. Peace and quiet are essential for concentration. Sideline chatter, excess use of voice or whip, all cause disturbance.

WORDS OF COMMAND

Words of command may be said to be the framework of instruction. They are not in themselves instructional, but they do enable instruction to proceed in an orderly fashion.

If you are inexperienced, the ability to give clear commands will greatly boost your confidence. The ride will be assured that you know what you want, and, as they respond, you will feel more in control of the situation, able to concentrate on teaching.

Speak slowly, clearly and just loud enough to be heard easily by every member of the ride. Always give your commands in plenty of time. Commands must never be sharp or sudden.

Commands state: WHAT is to be done — a change of pace or direction, or the commencement of a movement; WHO is to do it — e.g., whole ride, No 1 ride, leading file, or rider's name; and WHEN or WHERE it is to be done.

For transitions, to allow time for preparation, a preliminary command is given, e.g., 'Whole ride, prepare to trot.' Check quickly that all riders are preparing, e.g., 'Mary, shorten your reins.'

This is followed by the executive command 'Ride, ter-rot', on which all ponies should change pace simultaneously. Upward transitions are generally easier to achieve smoothly than downward ones, so a smarter reaction can be expected. Use a brisk command on a rising inflexion for the 'Ride, ter-rot'.

For downward transitions, 'Whole ride, prepare to walk.' Check that all are sitting to the trot, with lower leg in contact and quiet hands. There should be a definite pause to allow for this check, before saying 'Ride' — pause — 'walk'. Allow the inflexion to drop a little, but emphasise the final consonant. Check that the leading file does not act too abruptly.

Halting the ride and moving off

1. In the track. The quickest way in an emergency, or for a brief halt. *Commands:* 'Whole ride, prepare to halt, ride halt.' To move off, 'Whole ride, prepare to walk, ride walk on.'

2. On the long side. Use when inspecting the ride, or when demonstrating on the long side.

Commands: 'Leading file at M, turn in and halt 3m in from the track. Ride, form up on his left.'

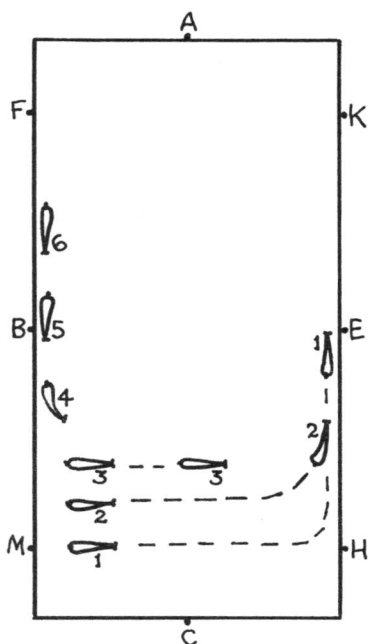

A ride turning in to line up on the long side. When moving off, No 1 leads, each subsequent rider moving straight forward in succession to turn left in the track and fit in at the correct distance.

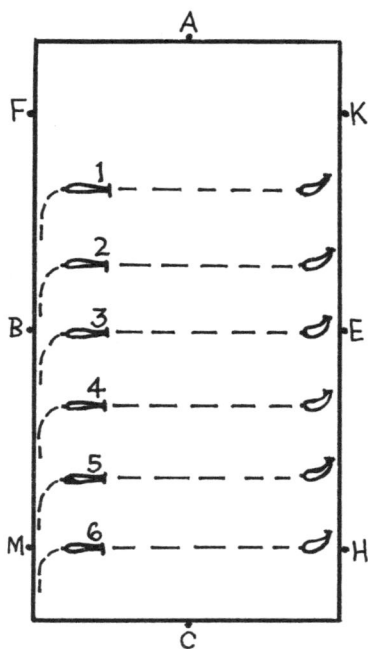

An alternative method. The whole ride turns in together and moves forward together. They must track the opposite way if ride order is to be maintained.

'In succession, behind your leader, walk on and track left (or right), leading file, walk on.'

'Whole ride, prepare to turn, ride, inwards turn and halt 3m in from the track.' A quicker method, but not feasible with a large ride.

'Whole ride, prepare to walk, ride, walk on and track right (left).'

3. Round the end of the school. Leaves both long sides and most of the school clear — useful for watching demonstrations or when working individually.

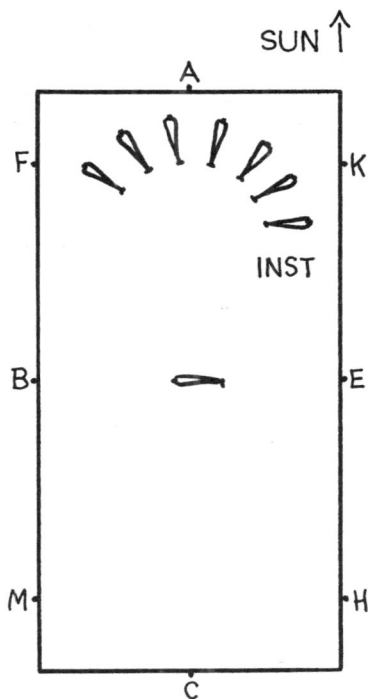

SUN ↑

The ride turned in at the end of the school, watching a demonstration of a 20m circle. Note backs to the sun.

Commands: 'At K, leading file inwards turn and halt 3m (10ft) in from the track, ride form up on his right round the end of the school.'

'In succession, behind your leader, walk on to M and change the rein. Leading file, walk on.'

Note: Wherever a ride is lined up, in the school or outside, all ponies must be level. It is most dangerous to allow some to stand half a length behind others.

Bringing the ride in 3m from the track gives sufficient space for individuals to go behind them safely.

Rides should not be lined up facing into the sun.

Riders should always move straight forward before making a turn.

SCHOOL EXERCISES AND COMMANDS

Exercises in single file
All movements must be carefully explained and demonstrated, and executed in walk until every member of the ride is sure of the track to be followed.

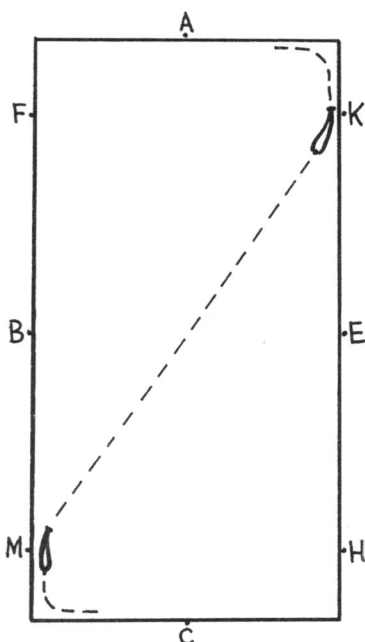

Change of rein, M to K.

1. Change of rein on the diagonal.

Command: 'Whole ride, in single file from M to K, incline.' The command must be given before the leading file reaches H.

Check: Each rider should begin the incline when his shoulder is level with M, and should aim to hit the track about a metre before K, so that his shoulder will be level with the marker as he straightens out before the corner. The whip should be changed, preferably before, but not during, the change of rein. Change the diagonal at the end of the movement — changing it at X makes it harder to keep the pony straight and is extremely disruptive if any lengthening is being asked for.

2. Turning down the centre.

Command: 'Whole ride, in single file, at A (or C), down the centre.' If a change of rein is required, add, 'and change'. The command should be given before the leader reaches the previous half-marker (B or E).

Check: Each rider should turn accurately on to the centre line, without overshooting and go straight. Looking at the ride from front or rear, you should see only one pony. Emphasise correct placing for the second turn.

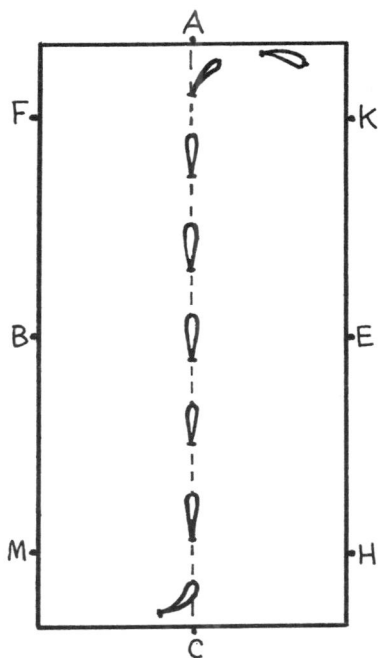

Turning down the centre. Good line, and the turning ponies are well placed.

3. Turning across the school.

Command: 'Whole ride, in single file at B (or E), right turn' ('and change', if required). Give the command before the leading file reaches A or C.

Check: Riders should turn before the pony's nose comes to the marker, otherwise they will overshoot the turn. Placing for both turns is most important.

Useful for practising turns at walk with beginners' rides, but should only be used occasionally at trot or ponies will begin to anticipate.

4. Circles.

Command: 'Whole ride, at A (C, B or E), on a 20m circle.' In trot, specify whether rising or sitting. Circles of less than 20m can only be performed in single file with small rides. To leave the circle, the command is 'Go large'.

Check: Shape of circle, aids, rhythm, bend. It is better not to ask for more than one circle at a time in trot, possibly two in walk, otherwise the natural tendency of ponies to fall in will be aggravated. While single-file work is useful initially for establishing shape, subsequent circles are better performed in succession or as individual exercises.

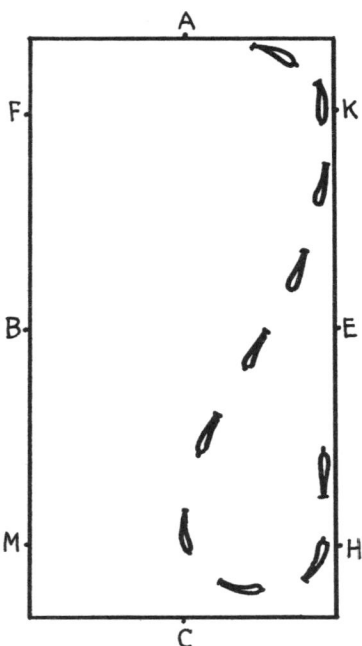

Half-circle and change the rein.

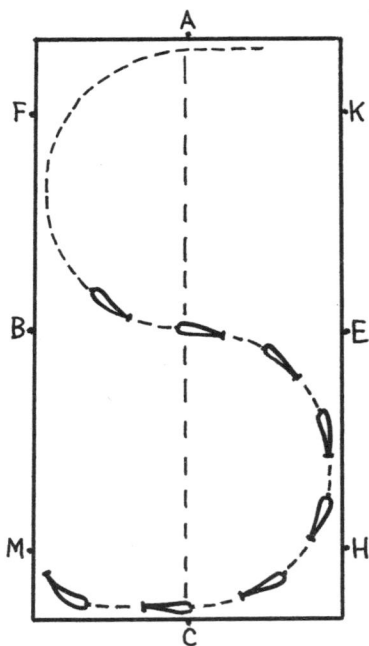

Half-circles AX–XC. Ponies should cross the centre line at right angles.

5. Half-circle and change the rein.
Command: 'Whole ride, in single file, at H, half-circle on to the centre line, returning to the track at K.'
Check: The size of the half-circle and the placing of the pony approaching K. Useful for introducing smaller circles, and as an alternative method of changing the rein.

6. Half-circles AX–XC or BX–XE.
Command: 'Whole ride, in single file, half-circle left A to X and half-circle right X to C.'
Check: The pony should be straight on or across the centre line between the two half-circles. At trot these exercises are best done individually or with the ride well spaced out.

7. Loop.
Command: 'Whole ride, in single file, between F and M, ride a loop of 5m (or 10m).'
Check: The smoothness of the changes of bend, and of the riders'

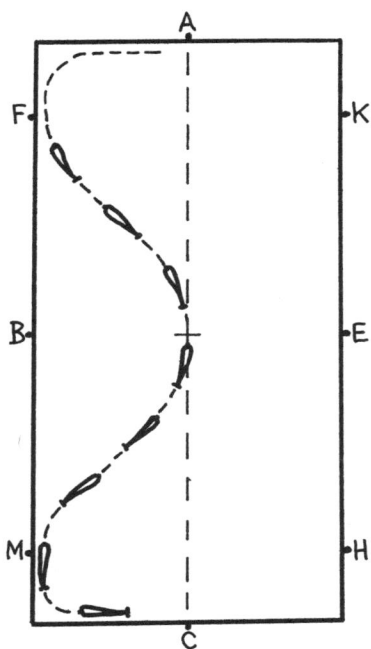

Loop. FXM. The bend is changed between F and X, and again between X and M. Less experienced rides should perform a shallower loop of 3 to 5m.

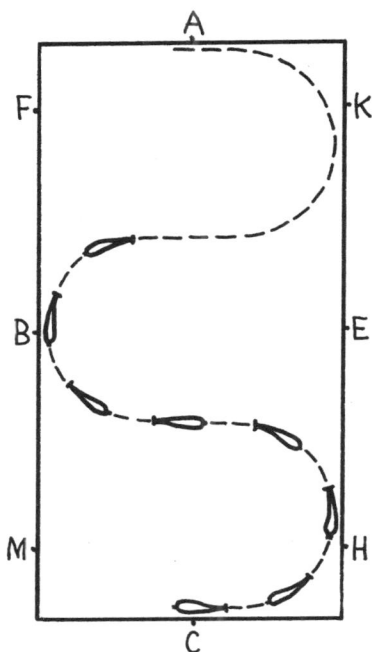

Three-loop serpentine.

aids, at the points marked. The whip need not be changed, nor the diagonal in rising trot.

8. Serpentine.
Command: 'Whole ride, in single file, at A (or C) ride a three-loop serpentine.'
Check: The shape and evenness of the loops and the smooth changes of bend. The whip is best kept on the pony's stiff side, the diagonal should be changed on the centre line.

Exercises in succession
1. Halting from the rear of the ride.
Commands: 'John, prepare to halt, and halt. Mary, prepare to halt,' etc. When all are halted, 'John, walk on, Mary, walk on,' etc.
Check: In halting: correct aids. The pony should halt with the minimum of resistance, and stand straight and still. In walking on:

49

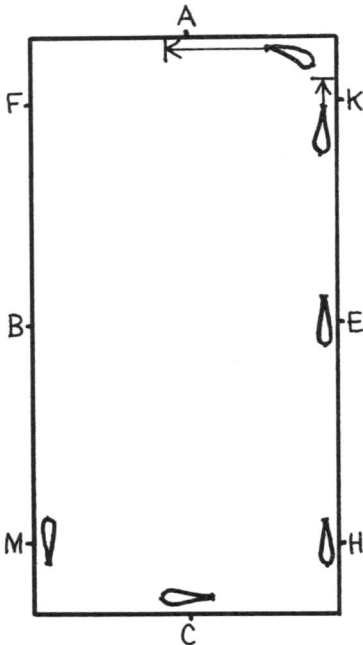

Halting from the rear of the ride at a given marker.

use of aids. Pony should move forward promptly from light leg aids. A good exercise for novice riders and young horses.

Or, slightly more difficult, halting at a given marker, as shown.
Commands: 'Halting from the rear of the ride at your next marker. Rear file, commence.' Commands to walk on, as above.
Check: As above, plus accuracy of halt — rider's shoulder level with marker.

2. Trot or canter from front to rear of the ride.
Commands: 'Trotting/cantering from front to rear of the ride. Leading file commence.' For subsequent riders it is only necessary to say 'Next'.
Check: In trot, that the rider sits for the first and last few strides of trot, and fits in correctly at the rear of the ride. Very useful at different levels for checking rider's position, rising or sitting trot, correct diagonals, pony's paces, and the transitions.

In canter, it is best done with the ride walking. The strike-off should be asked for in a corner with Pre-C riders or green horses. Seniors may be asked to strike-off from walk and/or on the long side.
Check: The placing of the pony and the aids for the canter strike-off. With juniors, tell them, or ask the next rider to tell them as the pony

50

strikes off, whether it is on the correct leg. If not, it should immediately be brought back to trot or walk, placing and aids re-checked, and the strike-off repeated in the next corner. Emphasise 'praise' the pony when correct. More experienced riders should tell you if the strike-off is correct.

Check: The rider's position and the pony's placing, rhythm and straightness in canter. That the rider starts steadying in time at the end of the exercise, to allow for a smooth transition through trot to walk, without bumping into or overtaking the rear file.

Note: Sitting trot on all transitions.

A useful variation is for the rider to continue past the ride on the inside (out of kicking distance) and to fit in the next time round. Excellent for making riders on lazy or nappy ponies use their legs. The whip is best in the outside hand.

This exercise is excellent for young horses, but not in canter.

3. Trot/canter from front to rear, with a circle at the free end of the school.

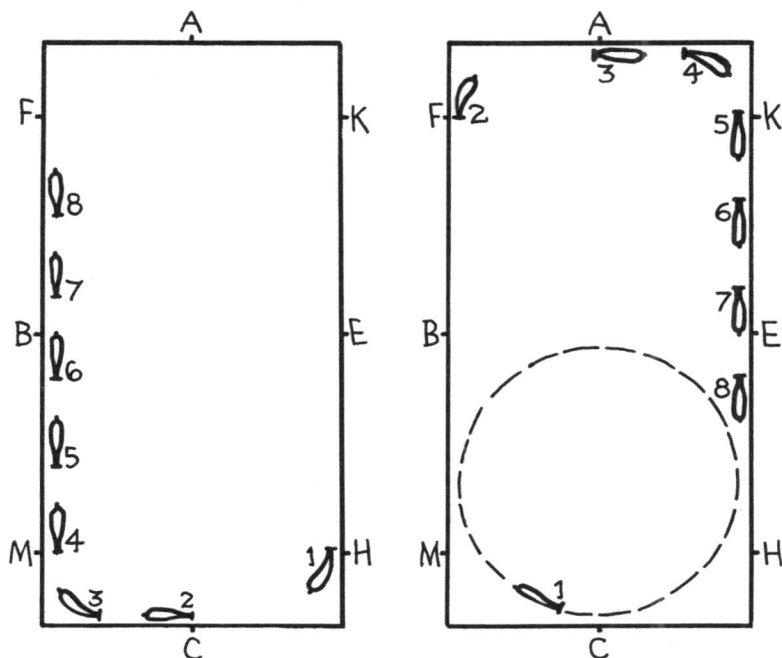

Trot/canter front to rear, with a circle at the free end of the school. No 1 started between C and H and will circle at C, No 2 is starting between A and F, to circle at A.

Commands: 'Trotting/cantering from front to rear of the ride, with a 20m circle at the free end of the school. Leading file commence, next,' etc. Specify whether rising or sitting trot. The rider makes one circle at A or C, whichever is free. All but advanced riders should be told where to circle.

Check: Position and aids, the transitions, the corners, the shape of the circle, maintenance of the pony's rhythm throughout and his bend on the circle.

More advanced riders may perform a 15 or 10m circle, commencing at B or E.

4. Circle from front to rear of the ride.
Commands: 'Circling from front to rear of the ride, leading file commence, next,' etc.
Check: Each rider should leave the side on a curve, not make a sharp turn. Once off the track, he should look over his inside shoulder at the rear file and judge the size of the circle so that he fits in one length behind, at approximately the point where he left the track, without altering the pace. The size of the circle will be governed by the number in the ride, so for rides of less than eight the spacing should be increased, otherwise they will have to make too small a circle.

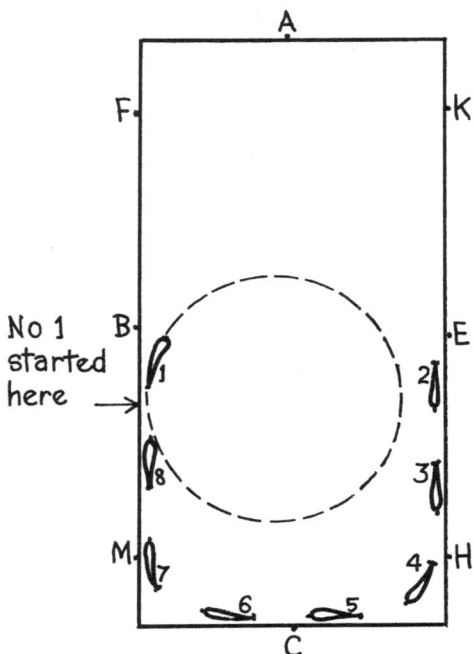

Circle front to rear. If the circle is to be round, it must finish where it started.

Start in walk — in trot, state whether the circle is to be in rising or sitting trot.

Good for teaching riders to look where they are going, and for developing judgment of pace and distance.

5. Leading files in succession down the centre, halt at D or G, then rejoin the rear of the ride.

Commands: This may be shortened to 'Leading files in succession down the centre — leading file commence'. Once the exercise is started, each new leader should automatically turn at the end of the school, halt at D or G, and fit in behind, so no further commands are needed.

Another invaluable exercise. For the rider, it gives practice in using the aids for turns and transitions; keeping the pony straight, on the line and at halt; leading the ride for a brief period; and keeping alert and thinking of the next move.

The pony learns to listen to the rider and do as he is told, leaving

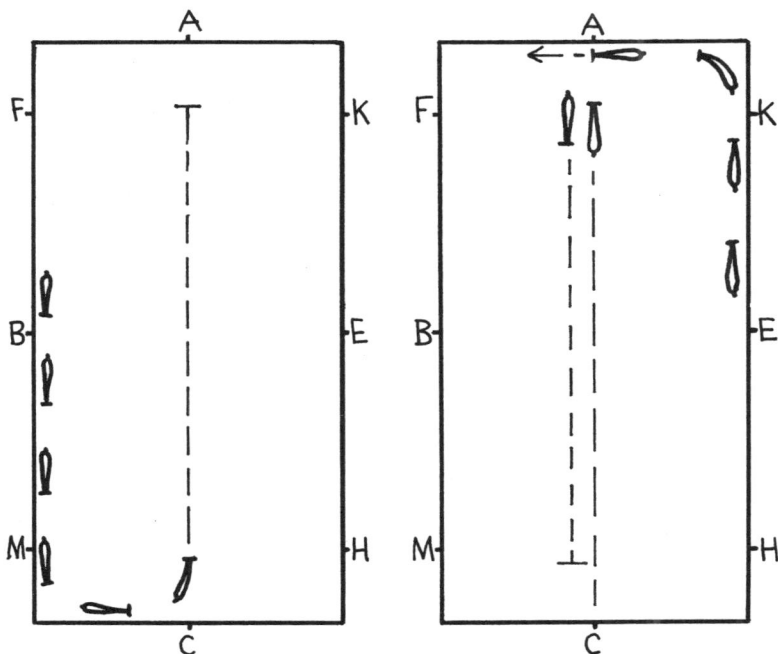

Leaders in succession up and down the centre. No 1 turned at C, and is standing waiting to fit in behind the rear file. No 2 turned round No 1, and will halt at G. *Note.* Only the odd numbers will be on the centre line — even numbers must remain parallel with it.

the ride to turn down the centre, but not automatically following the one in front; go on a straight line; stand still while others go past. It is especially useful for young horses.

Start at walk, and, for the first time or two, remind each rider when to turn, halt and move off. In trot, junior riders should walk at X, to avoid a rough or abrupt transition to halt.

Once the ride has grasped the exercise, the instructor, without the necessity of giving commands, should have ample time for constructive comments on each rider.

With all exercises in succession, it is essential that the ride maintains the required distance, and also that each leader maintains the same pace. Encourage riders to say if they feel the pace has altered.

FORMATION RIDING — DRILL WORK

Includes work in 'rides' and 'double ride'.

Many new instructors are wary of attempting this work because they feel it will be too complicated. Certainly it requires practice and concentration to time the commands correctly, but you will find, once you get into the swing of it, that it is satisfying for all concerned and engenders a fine team spirit.

The constant change of leaders within the rides, the need to work individually, yet together, to maintain distance and dressing, develop the quick reactions and the almost automatic application of aids so essential for active riding in the open.

Since this work is particularly suited to the Post-D to C+ range of riders — the majority group in Pony Club — all instructors are urged to study and make use of it.

Begin, if possible, by watching an experienced instructor taking the exercises. Try it out at home with matchsticks on a table.

First, divide the class. A class of eight divides into two fours, of ten into two fives. With nine riders, the obvious division is into three threes, or a five and a four may be easier.

Arrange the ride so that the weakest riders and any difficult ponies will be in the middle of their sections, where they will not be leaders at any stage. Try to have ponies of a similar size and length of stride in each section.

Preliminaries. Number the ride.

Commands: 'Ride, from the front, number.' The leading file turns his head over his inside shoulder and says, 'One,' the next, 'Two' and so on down the ride. It is often advisable to repeat this.

Then divide into rides as previously decided, e.g., 'Numbers 1 to

4 are Number 1 ride; numbers 5 to 8, Number 2 ride'. (It may be best to use 'Ride A' and 'Ride B', to avoid confusion with the riders' own numbers.)

Next, ask the ride to 'prove' that they know which ride they are in. On the command 'Ride A, prove,' each member of Ride A puts the reins into the outside hand and raises the inside arm, hand level with ear. Repeat this until you are sure everyone knows where they belong.

Exercises in rides

1. Turning across the school. (The easiest exercise to begin with.)
Commands: 'Ride A, left' (right, or inwards, if you prefer) — pause — 'turn.'

The pause gives the riders time to prepare, making the 'Ride A, left' act as a preliminary command. Riders must wait for the word 'turn', and act on it promptly when it comes. Then, 'Ride B, left — turn' and so on. The rides turn left automatically at the other side of the school — no further command is necessary. On a left turn, riders dress by the left — i.e., always keeping in line with the new leader.
Timing: It is essential to give the 'turn' command as the rear file of each section comes to the same spot — usually just past the first

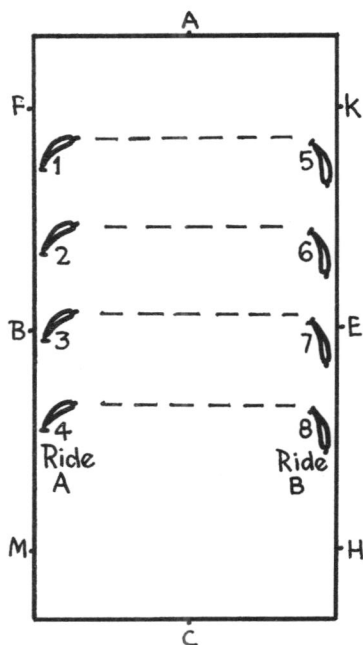

Left turns across the school, in rides of four. Each turn will change the ride order — No 4 becoming the leader of Ride A, No 8 the leader of Ride B.

55

quarter-marker on the long side — otherwise the spacing between sections will be lost.

Check: That the pace and distance are even, each section turning on the word, keeping dressing and straightness across the school so that they can turn together on the far side.

2. Turning across the school with a change of rein. (The second turn is to the opposite direction.)

Commands: 'Ride A, right — turn, and change, Ride B', etc. Rides dress by the left, as the second turn will be left.

Timing: The commands must be given earlier, as soon as the rear file of each section comes to the first quarter-marker on the long side, to allow room for the second turn.

Check: As above.

If things go wrong, don't panic! Make use of that invaluable command 'As you were'. Sort the ride back into their original order and try again. Establishing these exercises in walk is just as important for the instructor as it is for the ride.

With practice, you will begin to know almost instinctively when the next command is due, and will even have time to check individual rider's aids.

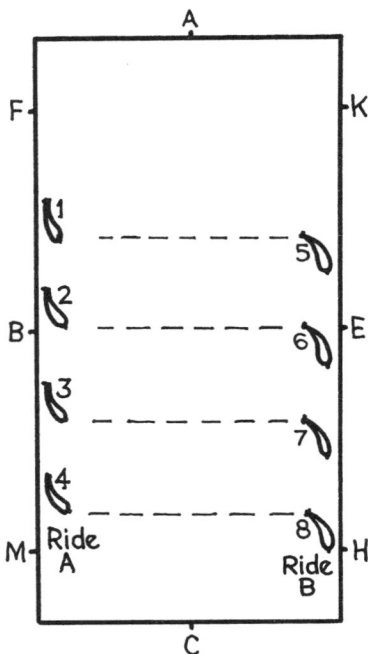

Left turn and change, in rides of four.
The ride order remains the same.

3. Inclining across the school. (Best done in rides of three.)
Commands: 'Inclining across the school in rides, Ride A, incline, Ride B, incline.'
Timing: Give the command 'Incline' as the rear file of each section comes to the first quarter-marker.
Check: That each section leader aims for the opposite quarter-marker, as for a change of rein. The ponies should be parallel and the riders' shoulders level during the incline.

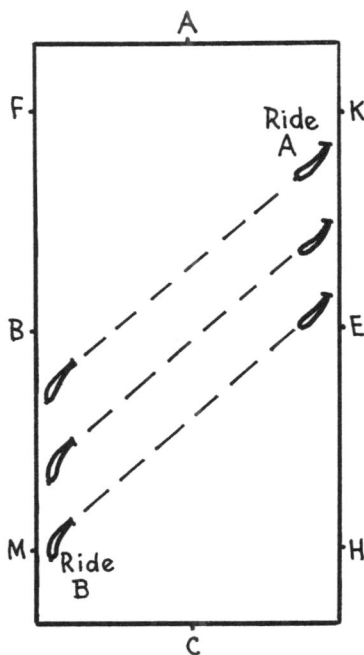

Inclining across the school in rides of three.

4. Half-circles on to the centre line and away. (Each ride makes individual half-circles on to the centre line and proceeds down the line, with the rear file in the lead, until it receives the command 'Away' when it half-circles back to the side.)
Commands: 'Half-circling on to the centre line, Ride A, commence, Ride B, commence, Ride A, away, Ride B, away.'

5. Half-figure of eight. (The rides go 'away' in the opposite direction — i.e., first half-circle left, second half-circle right.)
    These exercises are more difficult — considerable practice is needed in walk to ensure that everybody rides well-shaped half-circles.

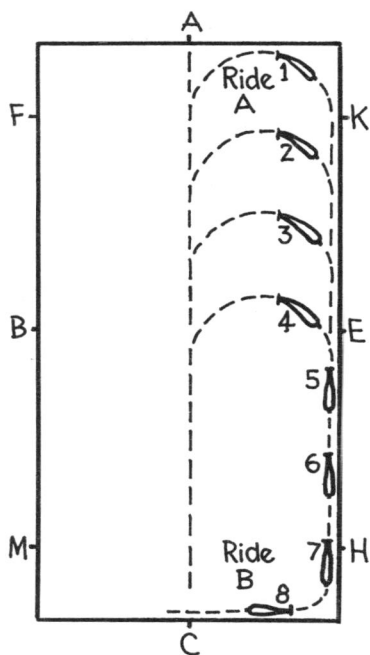

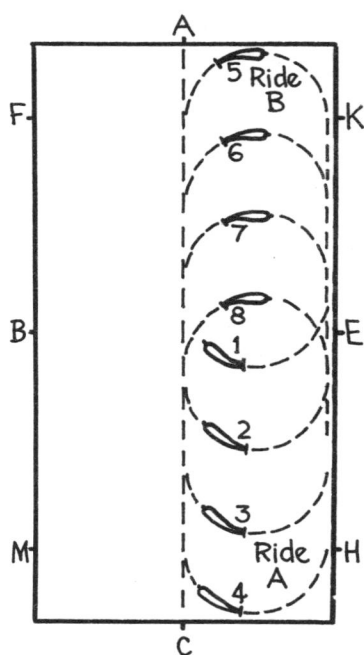

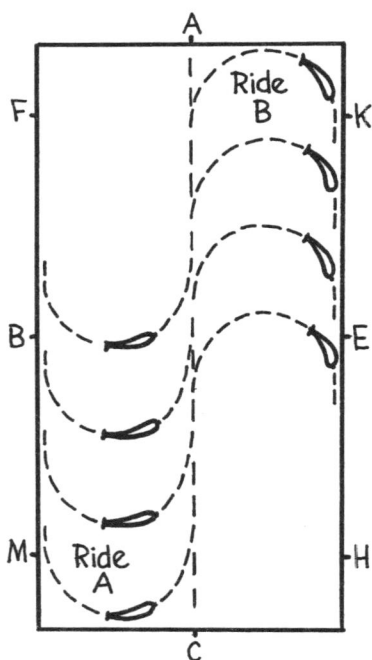

Above: Half-circles on to the centre line, in rides of four. (**A**) Ride A has started their half-circle. (**B**) Ride A has just received the command 'Away' and is returning to the long side. Ride B is commencing their half-circle on to the centre line.

Left: Half-figure of eight, commencing on the left rein. Ride A is going 'Away' to the right.

6. Full circles on to the centre line. (For more advanced rides.)
Commands: 'Circling on to the centre line, Ride B, commence,' then, on the next long side, 'Ride A, commence'.
Timing: Ride B must circle first, otherwise they will collide with Ride A.

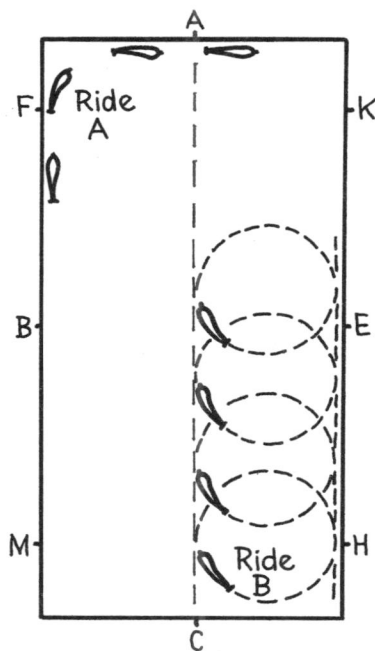

Full circles on to the centre line. Note that Ride B is circling first — Ride A will circle on the next long side.

Many more variations are possible — for instance, half-circles on to the centre line, then inclining away, either to the same side or to the opposite side.

Double ride
The ride will be divided into two sections, each following its own leading file. Choose two competent riders for Nos 1 and 2.

Number the ride, odd and even numbers 'prove'. See page 55.
Command: 'Whole ride in single file, down the centre, odd numbers to the right, even numbers to the left.' You will now have two rides on opposite reins — they pass left hand to left hand when they meet. Riders will be double distance apart, and must maintain this spacing. The even numbers dress opposite the spaces between the odd numbers for most exercises. The odd-numbered ride is responsible for the pace, the even-numbered for the dressing.

1. Turning across the school.

Command: 'Double ride, inwards — turn.' Unless a change of rein is ordered, each ride dresses to its new leader, on the side to which it has turned. The rides will cross on the centre line.

2. Changing the rein on the diagonal (scissors). (Distance and dressing must be correct, or there will be collisions.)

Command: 'Double ride, inclining across the school, leading files, incline.' The rides cross at X, Number 1 leader first, even numbers passing through the gaps. Looks most effective when well done.

3. Half-circles on to the centre line.

Command: 'Double ride, half-circling on to the centre line, commence.' Both rides circle inwards to the centre line, fitting into the gaps between riders and proceeding down the centre line in single file until commanded 'Away', when they each circle back to their original long sides. This method may also be used for a half-figure of eight.

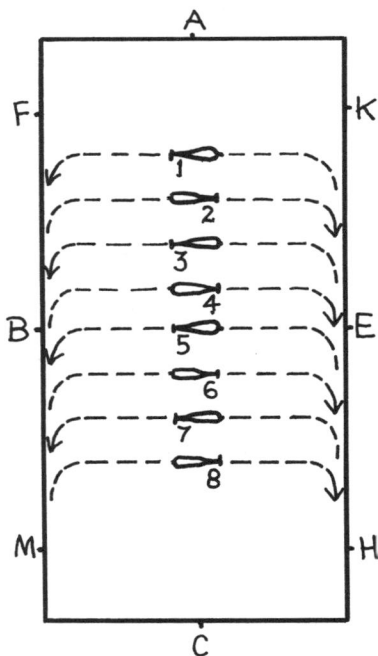

Double ride, inwards turn. Odd numbers turning left, even numbers right.

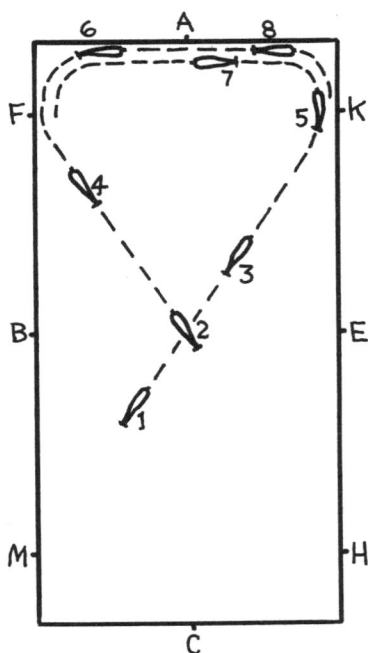

'Scissors.' Note rides passing left hand to left hand. No 1 passes in front of No 2.

60

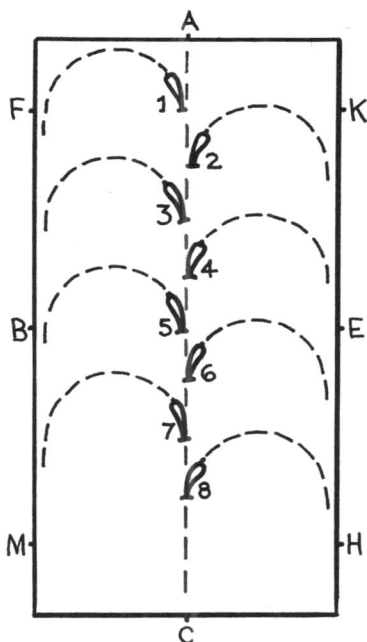

Right: Double ride, half-circles on to the centre line, with riders fitting in to come down the centre in single file.

Below: Double ride, half-circles on to the centre line, meeting in pairs. Obviously impossible for a half-figure of eight.

Below right: Double ride, 20m circles at A and C. If the dressing is correct, with odd numbers ahead of the even numbers, riders should dovetail at X, without collisions. The instructor should stand at E or B.

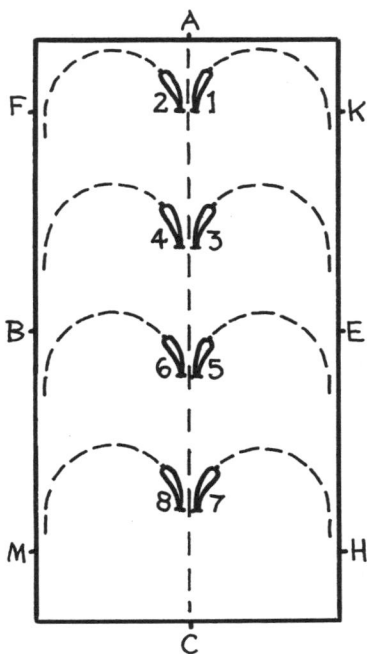

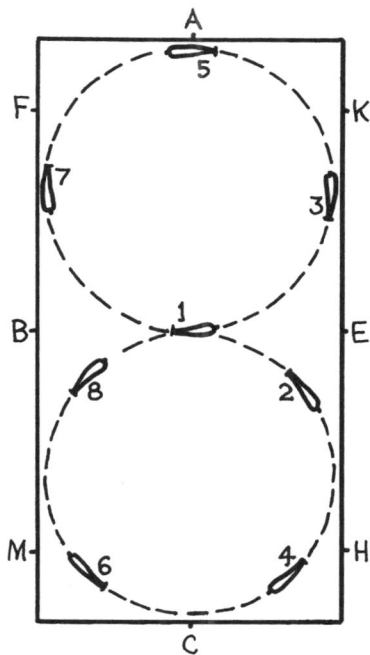

61

Double rides may also be worked with the odd and even numbers level, when the rides dress opposite to one another throughout. The rides can then turn up the centre in pairs, turning away in their pairs at the opposite end and continuing round the school. Excellent training in control, as, in order to maintain dressing, the inside rider must hold back and the outside one push on a little on the corners. Changes of rein on the diagonal and 20m circles may be carried out in pairs. Turning down the centre, inclining away from X to opposite quarter-markers and meeting again to turn down the centre is another good exercise.

The 'Cavalry Charge'
Based on a form of cavalry drill, this ride has been popular with all age-groups at Pony Club for many years. It may be carried out at walk even by beginners' rides, with unmounted assistance as needed. The procedure is as follows:
1. Number the ride — see page 54.
2. Whole ride in single file down the centre.
3. Odd numbers to the right, even numbers to the left.
4. Down the centre in pairs.
5. Pairs alternately right and left.
6. Down the centre in fours.

In a wide arena it is possible to continue on these lines until the riders come down the centre in eights or even sixteens.

To 'unwind' from here, eights or fours wheel right and left at the end of the school, then turn down the centre in fours or pairs. Pairs or single riders turn right or left, then down the centre in single file and turn right or left as a ride at the end of the school. The odd-numbered pairs or riders turn in front of the even numbers.

An alternative method is to halt the ride at X, then lead off in pairs or in single file in the original order. This can make a good finish to a musical ride.

Once they know the form of this ride, Pre-C to C+ riders will enjoy performing it in trot, but it should not be attempted in canter with rides below a good B standard.

If space is available and all ponies are under control, the real 'cavalry charge' can take place, with the whole ride galloping off in line abreast. Much enjoyed by riders and ponies alike.

As you and your ride become more familiar with all these exercises, you will doubtless think of endless combinations and variations. It can be good fun (and quite a salutary experience for them) to allow members of the ride to command the movements, to help them to appreciate the importance of timing and accuracy.

Tricycling

This is a type of formation riding in sections of three, based on the 'turns across the school' on page 55, with which all must be familiar.

On the command 'Commence tricycling' the leader rides the corners in the normal way, but Nos 2 and 3, instead of following, turn with him, cross the school abreast and turn in the same direction on the far side, so that they revert to single file, in reverse order.

The exercise is repeated at both ends of the school, each subsequent section turning in the same way until the command 'Cease tricycling' is given.

Once the ride has grasped the basic principle of these repeated turns, other movements may be added, such as inclining across the school, 20m circles, half-figure of eight on to the centre line, always in threes. The leading trio chooses the movements, the others follow on. It will be noticed that each rider always follows in the track of the person three places ahead — i.e., 4 follows 1, 5 follows 2, 6 follows 3, and so on.

This is a useful method of working a large ride of C to B standard, provided that all are familiar with the movements you wish to include. It obviates the necessity for continual commands, leaving the instructor free to concentrate on teaching, while everyone in the ride must be alert and attentive in order to keep his place. Successful tricycling gives a great sense of teamwork. Set to music, it can make a simple but effective form of musical ride, requiring a minimum of rehearsal and no commands.

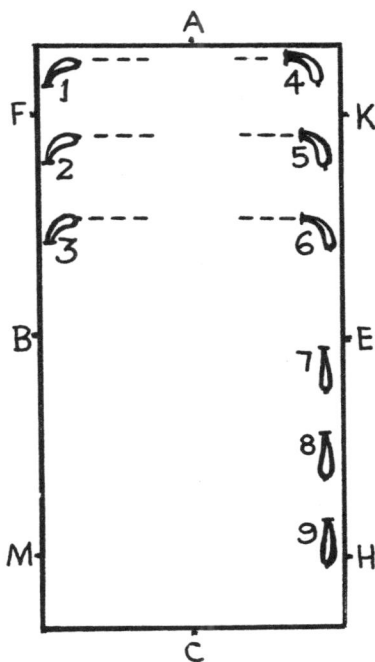

Tricycling. Turning in threes at the end of the school. Note how the section order changes with each turn, but Nos 4 and 7 always follow No 1, Nos 5 and 8 follow No 2, and so on.

MUSICAL AND ACTIVITY RIDES

A musical ride is basically a formation ride to music, generally in a large arena 60 by 30m, or longer, according to the number taking part. It is easiest with multiples of four. Trot is usually the predominant pace, and the most suitable for C riders.

An activity ride, as the name implies, is generally a more athletic affair, and may include trotting poles, cavalletti, physical exercises on the flat or over jumps or vaulting. It will probably be performed mostly in canter, and will require a higher degree of fitness in ponies and riders. Music adds interest and helps the timing.

All participants, riders and ponies, should be familiar with the exercises in rides and double ride work on pp 54–62. Spacing and dressing must be accurately maintained.

Ponies/horses should be free but calm, reasonably even in size and length of stride, and it certainly looks more impressive if those in each section can be matched in colour.

Producing a musical or activity ride

Start by working out the pattern of the ride. It must fill the arena with movement throughout, and include turns, circles and inclines for the varied patterns they provide. Riding in single file, pairs or fours also adds variation.

When you have what appears to be a satisfactory outline, write it down in movements, as for a dressage test. Musical rides generally vary from about eight to twelve minutes' duration, and an eight minute ride will comprise about 30 movements, twelve minutes up to 40, as a rough guide.

Next, try it out with a small group, make any necessary alterations and time the whole exercise. Have everything as well planned as possible before trying it out with the full ride.

Explain the concept of the ride, then work through it one or two movements at a time in walk. When everyone is clear about the pattern and sequence, proceed to trot.

Even with rides that are capable of working in canter, the movements must be thoroughly established first in the slower paces, and before setting it to music.

Jumps in activity rides must always be small, so that ponies will 'pop' over them in their stride, without breaking the rhythm. Cavalletti are most useful because they are easy to move and do not obscure the view of spectators. In an arena, jumps may be set on the long sides or just in from them, on the centre line or on the diagonal. An 'arena party' of members, suitably dressed in Pony Club uniform, may be needed to move them during the ride. For early practices use poles on the ground.

Jumping in pairs or in fours, holding a ribbon between the riders, looks effective, as does negotiating a 'box' of cavalletti, placed diagonally either side of X, in a scissors formation. Individual exercises may be performed in succession, giving scope for variation according to the ability of the riders.

It is a moot point whether or not rides should be commanded. If there is only a limited time available for rehearsal — as, for instance, with a ride produced as a display for an Open Day at the end of a week in camp — commands will be essential, but they lessen the appearance of spontaneity.

Music

The tempo of the music must suit the pace. The walk goes to 2/4 time, trot to 4/4, canter to 6/8. Military marches are particularly suitable for trot, Irish jigs and Scottish reels for canter. Country and western, Bavarian music and numbers from musicals, can all be useful.

A mounted 'square dance' can be great fun. The calls take the place of formal commands.

Dress

This may be Pony Club uniform, or it could be period or military costume. If members are capable of riding with one hand, wooden 'lances' with different coloured pennants for each section look most effective.

In fact, the only limiting factors are the imagination and ingenuity of the person designing the display. Always remember that a simple programme, well executed, is more effective than an over-ambitious muddle.

TAKING RIDES FOR JUMPING

This section includes safety factors, building confidence, improving the partnership.

Safety

1. Check that the paddock gate is shut.
2. Check or re-check all tack — fitting of helmets, girths, saddles, stirrup-irons or bridles if changed for jumping, martingales. Knot reins which could catch on rider's foot with shorter stirrups.

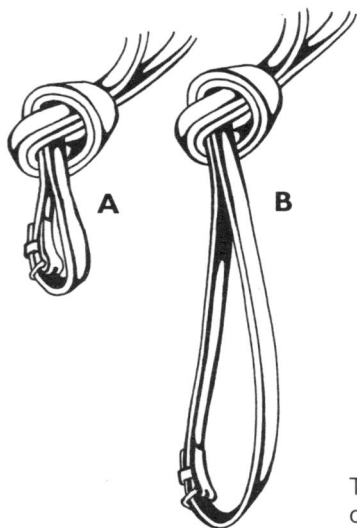

Tie knot in the *end* of reins that may catch on the rider's foot. (**A**) Correct. (**B**) Incorrect.

3. Have neckstraps for beginners, nervous riders and those on young or difficult ponies/horses.

4. Never have empty top cups on stands, or use rough, sharp or cracked poles. Check all filling for safety.

5. Keep order, control the pace. Make it a rule that everybody returns to their place at walk, preferably on a long rein, after their turn at jumping.

Confidence of rider and pony

1. Aim from the very beginning to establish control and calmness. The ability to achieve a correct approach at a given pace in itself gives great confidence.

2. Always start at a height well within the ability of the weakest member, rider or pony. Allow time for the partnership to establish an exercise thoroughly before increasing the degree of difficulty.

3. Jumping in single file — follow-my-leader style — with a good, steady leader, or a lead from another pony, will encourage the sluggish or uncertain, but should not be overdone.

4. Jumping without reins, sensibly conducted, can give great confidence to riders, and even more to ponies, who know that their mouths won't be hurt.

5. Never attempt to force any riders to jump against their wishes, but try to find out quietly what is at the root of their reluctance.

Children who are not very keen on jumping should be encouraged to develop their capabilities without pressure. They should be expected to ride over ground poles as part of regular work, even if led, and should remain with the ride to watch the jumping. They may be encouraged to ride a 'course' round some of the fences, or over poles on the ground between stands. Often, after a few weeks, they will suddenly gain confidence and begin to enjoy themselves. Be extra careful not to overface.

Those who do not jump at all miss out on a lot of fun and camaraderie at Pony Club.

6. Build good fences and courses. Good distances in combinations and gymnastic exercises build confidence, bad ones destroy it and can be dangerous. See page 69.

7. The instructor must be prepared — and must have help — to alter fences according to ability, and, for combinations, length of stride. Jumping rides should be as even as possible in both respects. If the group is mixed, more experienced riders must be given the chance to work over more difficult problems.

8. Always praise the rider generously for good work, and make sure that this praise is passed on to the pony. Appreciation builds confidence in both.

Improvement in the partnership

1. Establish aims for all members of your ride. Most riders want to compete at some level and/or pass certificates, and therefore need to learn to ride a course of fences competently. This is the real fun in jumping, but it still requires constant work on the basics to achieve and maintain standards.

2. Good jumping is dependent on sound work on the flat. One of the principal tasks of the jumping instructor is to help pupils to understand and appreciate the value of dressage in achieving the balance and control necessary for successful jumping.

USE OF EQUIPMENT

Trotting poles

1. Single, 'scattered' poles. For teaching riders to look and think ahead, aiming at right angles to the centre of each pole and going straight 'before, over and after' — a prerequisite for successful jumping. Also excellent for young horses, and for keeping excitable ones guessing.

2. Three poles approximately 2.4 to 2.7m (8 to 9ft) apart, according to length of stride. Best placed in the open, with space to circle either

way. Will fit in with either walk or trot, and so form an excellent follow-on from the above. Ponies will usually stretch more in walk, enabling the rider to feel this more clearly.

3. Four to six poles at half the above distance. These are not suitable for walking, and should be used only in trot. 1.2 to 1.37m (4ft to 4ft 6in) is generally correct for ponies, but small ponies may need an even shorter distance. See *Manual No 2*, page 66, for adjusting poles for individuals. If sizes are mixed, use two sets of poles side by side.

See *Manual No 1*, page 82, and *Manual No 2*, page 65, for uses of trotting poles for both rider and horse/pony.

Poles on the ground or cavalletti form a useful part of the work-in, at all levels. When working as a ride, horses should be not less than four lengths apart. The emphasis for the rider should be on straightness, both in his position and in the track taken over the poles, and on maintaining contact, while allowing the horse to take all the rein it needs.

The horse must be calm, keep a soft, even pace, and bend correctly when circling.

Jumping, cantering or scrambling through the poles will do more harm than good. Check that the distance is suitable, insist on a very steady pace, work individually if necessary.

When the stride is established through the poles, look for use of head and neck, rounding the back.

4. A small jump beside the trotting poles allows practice over poles and jump alternately.

5. Poles as above, followed by a small jump, double distance. Excellent for establishing the jumping position, emphasising a calm approach in stride, and improving the rider's contact and the horse's style of jumping.

Adding another jump gives a one-stride double or a bounce. Good for excitable horses, and helping those who have problems in adjusting their stride, provided the distance is right for them. See below.

Fences

At all levels, fences must be correctly built, with plenty of variation. See *Manual No 1*, pages 86–88, and *Manual No 2*, pages 61–65.

For beginners, human or equine, fences should consist of two poles, crossed or horizontal with dropper or ground-line. Crossed poles encourage the horse to make for the middle, the lowest point. Spreads or more complicated-looking obstacles would be likely to cause ponies to 'spook', or to jump very big.

As height increases, more poles will be needed — approximately one for every 30cm (1ft), so a 60cm (2ft) fence will usually require three poles. If short of poles, a dropper may be used up to 90cm (3ft). Never use two widely spaced poles with no ground-line, or a single pole.

Spreads

The easiest type consists of crossed poles with ground-line and a horizontal on the landing side. See *Manual No 1*, page 88, or *Manual No 2*, page 69. From this, go to an ascending oxer or hog's back. Small, true parallels or double crossed poles may be used when the fence is to be jumped both ways.

Filling

Once the ride is jumping freely over simple pole jumps up to about 45cm (18in), filling should be introduced, so that pony and rider become accustomed to every type of obstacle in miniature. For ideas, see *Manual No 1*, pages 87–88. With the drums, bales, etc., make a gap in the middle with just a pole on the ground and, with an experienced pony leading, let the whole ride follow on at trot through the gap. Repeat until all are going freely, then raise the pole, and finally fill the gap.

Large (44-gallon) drums should only be used on their sides. They must not have open ends and need rails or blocks to stop them rolling. Standing upright, these drums are dangerous for jumping.

Combinations

See *Manual No 1*, page 88, and *Manual No 2*, pages 68–70 and 186.

Distance is always measured from inside element to inside element of each fence. The smaller the fences in a combination, the less distance will be required between them. Overlong distances tend to encourage speed and flat jumping.

Distances should be adjusted to suit the stride of horse/pony as well as the height and type of fences. When this is not possible, as in a competition, always use the 'horse' distance. If ridden steadily, ponies can put in an extra stride, but horses may injure themselves if the fences are too close.

Two-stride doubles are the easiest for beginners or young horses. Initially, the first element should be crossed poles, not more than 30cm (1ft) in the centre, and the second an upright, with ground-line or dropper. This encourages a straight jump in, and a free jump out. Change to two small uprights, then make the first element an inviting spread.

Starting at a height of about 30 to 45cm (1 to 1ft 6in), 9.1m (30ft) should give two comfortable 'round' strides for ponies, with the approach in canter, and for horses in trot. In canter, use 9.7m (32ft) for horses.

For one-stride doubles use the same sequence of fences. With very small jumps, distances will vary from about 5.4 to 6.1m (18ft to 20ft). In this case they must be altered according to size of horse/pony, though some slight adjustment can be made by moving the ground-line or bringing out the base of the dropper on the second fence.

For bounces (no strides in between) begin with two crosses, about 30cm (1ft) in centre. Jump in succession, with a free pony in front. Change second element to horizontal pole with dropper, repeat. Trot round, canter last few strides. Hand on neck or neckstrap for any who are unsteady. Then make two small uprights, the second fractionally higher. Do not use spreads in the early stages. Distance 2.7 to 3m (9 to 10ft) approximately. With mixed rides, to save altering distances, it is acceptable to have horses trot and ponies canter the last few strides.

JUMPING AND GYMNASTIC EXERCISES

All distances between poles and fences must be adjusted to suit the strides of horses and ponies. See *Manual No 2*, pages 67–69 and 184–185.

These exercises will be introduced from about Stage Pre-C+. Valuable as they are for developing the rider's eye and the horse's agility, exercises involving several fences in line are not suitable for mixed rides. Following gymnastic exercises the lesson should finish over two or three easy, free-going fences.

COURSES

In training, the aim is to teach riders to take a smooth track from one fence to another. Courses should include some fences in a straight line, others before or after a turn, with at least one change of direction. The track should be designed in such a way that the horse can maintain a regular stride, can approach each fence without deviation and is not expected to change the canter lead continually.

Approaches and turns
Two fences in line teach riding straight and allow every chance to maintain an even stride and balance. Possible excess speed can be governed by a following turn.

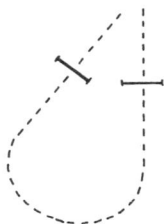

Fences in line.   A dogleg.   A good schooling turn.   A U-turn.

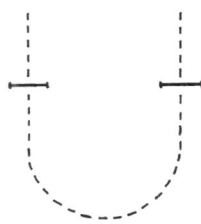

A dogleg is difficult, as it disrupts the stride. It should never be used between the first two fences, before a combination or for riders below C+ to B standard.

Fences set close together at an angle of 140 degrees approximately, are educational for novice riders and easy for green horses. Markers may be used, as shown, to help the inexperienced to ride a correct 'track'.

U turns can be severe if the fences are too close together, 20m (66ft) would be the minimum distance in most cases.

Fences set at, or close to, right angles, require controlled and calculated riding, and help to steady pace. It must always be possible to ride smoothly from one to the other without pulling out to make room. As a guide, allow a minimum of three strides 14m (46ft) after landing from the first fence, three strides for the turn, and three strides for the approach to the second fence.

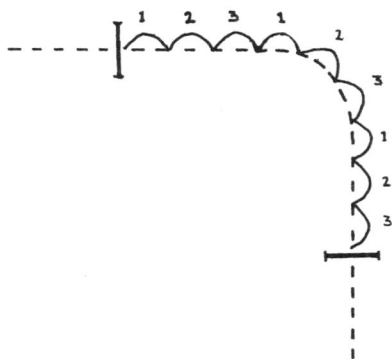

A well-placed right angle.   Too tight!

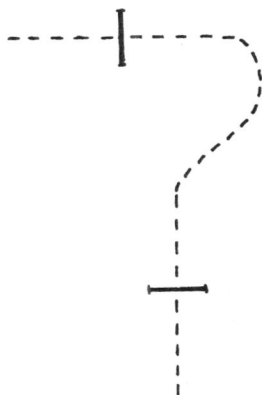

Always allow at least two single fences before a combination, and ample room for the approach.

If the ground is not completely flat, special care will be needed to site fences safely. Show-jumping combinations should not be jumped downhill.

It is generally best to keep training courses fairly short — four to seven fences. It should be possible to build a course that, with minor alterations, can be adapted to suit all levels at a rally.

Manual No 1 (1988 edition), pages 86 and 88, and *Manual No 2*, pages 67 and 71, show other useful layouts.

If the ride is mixed, start at the lowest level, with the fences set accordingly. This allows for those who have a clear round to have their second round over fences set for the next level, and so on.

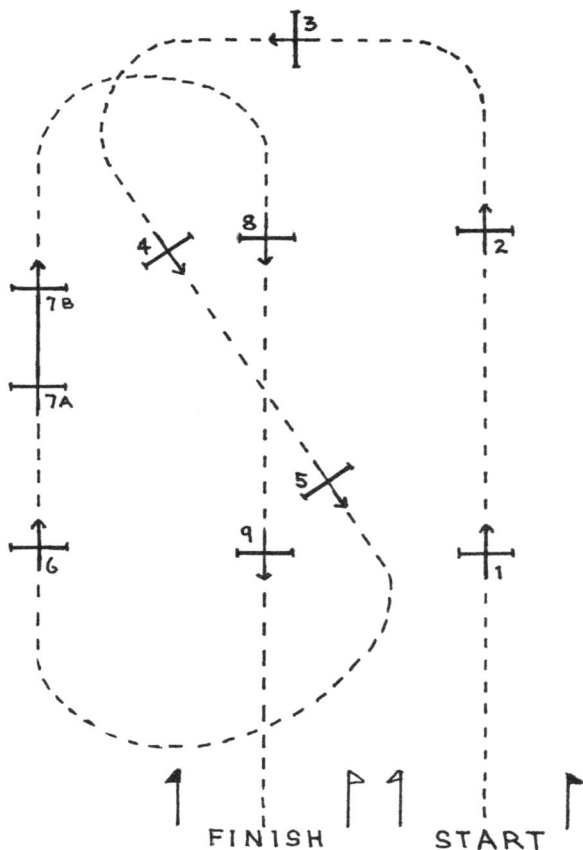

A flowing course, which could be adapted to suit most levels.

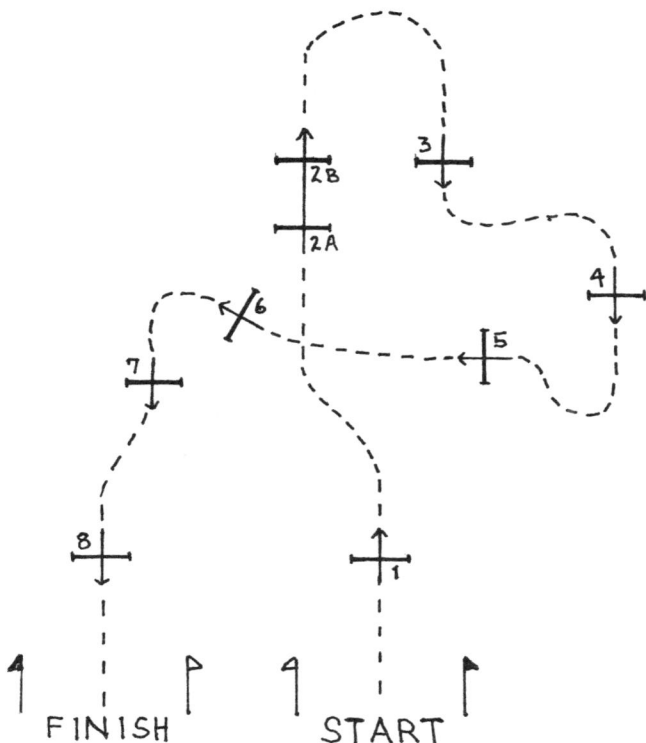

Some of the 'no-noes'. Dogleg between 1 and 2, double too soon, impossible turns, no chance to establish rhythm.

It is usually best for each rider to have two rounds, to improve or consolidate on the first effort.

If one or two fences were jumped badly, check briefly with the rider, who should repeat those fences only, before returning to the ride. If all were jumped badly, re-think the situation. Why?

Those who do a really good first round may have fences enlarged, at the instructor's discretion.

It can be worthwhile to have each rider jump one or two successive fences, round the course, before tackling it as a whole.

Pairs of markers on the approach and landing side of a fence or on turns round a course can help novice riders to go straight and ride a good line. Removing the obstacles and riding between the stands, or walking the course on foot, are other useful exercises.

Jumping without reins
This is one of the best ways of developing an independent seat, and is greatly enjoyed by most riders. It is amazing how quietly even the most excitable ponies will jump once they realise that they have complete freedom of head and neck over the fence.

A small bounce is excellent for this. Procedure is as follows:

1. Close in the sides with poles. Ensure that ponies will be jumping away from 'home' — i.e., the paddock gate.

2. Jump several times in succession, with reins, to familiarise.

3. Riders knot reins short, on pony's neck. They must not drop the reins without this knot. Whips should be handed in.

4. Riders jump individually, approach in trot, canter last few strides, or in last stride only for bigger horses. Drop reins about 3m (10ft) out, put both hands on neck. Pick up reins and guide pony straight on after landing. After the first attempt, especially if riders show signs of tension, encourage them to make animal noises, sing a song or count 'one, two' as the pony jumps. Demonstrate.

5. When all are confident and keeping a good position, use different hand positions — hands on knees, holding (rider's!) ears, flying angels (*Manual No 1*, page 89), clapping as you count over the jumps, 'boxer's handshake'. In the early stages, don't use hands behind the back, as it could cause novice riders to be left behind.

6. Always finish with one or two jumps with reins to check improvement in positions and riders' contact.

Jumping without stirrups is excellent for improving balance and strengthening the seat, but it demands a fair degree of physical fitness in the rider. It is therefore generally unsuitable for rides below Stage Pre-B3 level. Reins should be knotted and dropped and exercises carried out as above. Horses must be calm and sensible.

For further details of jumping instruction at different levels, and for cross-country training, see Chapters 4, 5, 6 and 8.

Other mounted instruction
Road safety training — Chapter 4, page 115.
Riding up and down hill — Chapter 4, page 115.
Opening and shutting gates — Chapter 4, page 117.
Speed and distance training — Chapter 5, page 134.
Games — Chapters 3, 4 and 5.

UNMOUNTED INSTRUCTION

Horse/pony management
The practical lesson is by far the best. It enables the instructor to instil or confirm good habits in handling, tying-up, leading, etc., and the use of correct terminology.

Requirements:

1. A quiet and comfortable place for the class to sit, where all can see and hear easily. Shade or shelter, according to weather conditions.

2. A quiet pony, correctly tied up and suitably presented for the purpose required. A cover if necessary. A haynet can help to keep the pony still.

Make sure the pony will do whatever is required — e.g., pick up feet, have bridle put on and taken off, load on to a float — try beforehand with the actual float you will be using. If you intend to demonstrate veterinary procedures — bandaging, hosing, taking a temperature — be sure the pony is familiar with the procedure.

Sometimes several ponies may be required, either for comparison of condition or conformation, or to allow more people to practise at the same time — e.g., bandaging. The above conditions apply to all. At times, all the ponies belonging to the ride may be tied up nearby, so that all can practise grooming, saddling, etc.

3. A drop skep or barrow and shovel will be needed, so that droppings can be picked up immediately and the area kept clean.

4. Props as required. See page 78.

Lessons on saddlery, feeding, etc., are ideally given in the appropriate place — a well-appointed tack or feed room — where this is possible.

The lesson will follow a similar pattern as for riding (see page 37).

1. Preparation.

2. Explanation.

3. Demonstration, combined with explanation to maintain interest and ensure understanding. A long, silent demonstration of grooming, for example, will mean nothing. If you can't talk and 'do' at the same time, use a well-briefed assistant to help.

4. Invite questions.

5. Practice. Singly, in small groups or together, according to circumstances. Sometimes in pairs, one doing, the other holding the pony and otherwise assisting, then changing places. The instructor and assistant watch and comment overall.

6. Re-demonstrate and explain, as required.

7. Further practice.
8. Prove the lesson.
Keep the lesson short, maintain interest.

The horse-management workshop is a useful method of teaching, particularly of revising prior to tests, and of splitting up a large class, ensuring involvement and variety for all.

Several points are set up, each with pony and/or props, and an instructor or assistant. Suitable subjects would be grooming, tack cleaning, bandaging, etc. The class is divided into groups of not more than six, which move from point to point to practise each task.

Associate or older members, who hold at least C+ Certificate, can make excellent assistants, or class members can take it in turns, under supervision, to act as instructors or demonstrators.

Lectures have the disadvantage that they may become too theoretical, too long and too school-like, especially for younger members. However, they are essential for teaching subjects such as the principles of feeding and conditioning, some aspects of health care and the theoretical side of riding. It is up to the instructor to make them interesting and memorable. The following suggestions may help:
1. Research and organise your material carefully — relate it to the age and experience of the ride. Cut out everything that does not contribute to the subject. Write short headings on cards.
2. Plan to incorporate visual aids. See page 78. These are essential to bring your lecture to life.
3. Your talk must have a beginning, a middle and an end. It can be helpful to memorise your opening and closing sentences.

First state your subject, how it relates to the class, and how knowledge of it will benefit riders and their ponies. Develop the points on your card-headings in sequence, finish by summing up the main points and offering a conclusion. Don't bring in new material near the end.
4. Practise and time your talk beforehand. A tape-recorder can help in checking delivery.
5. Make sure the class is comfortably settled where all can see and hear. Confirm both at the beginning.
6. Be comfortable yourself, standing or sitting, whichever way you feel most at ease.
7. Speak slowly enough for each point to be absorbed. Avoid addressing one person continually, but establish eye contact with different members of the class in turn — especially the shy or the disruptive.
8. Speak with conviction. If you feel strongly about a subject (e.g.,

ponies wintering in horse-sick, windswept paddocks with no supplementary feed) don't hesitate to say so.

9. Be sincere and natural. Beware of cliches, such as 'at this point in time' when you mean 'now'. Keep sentences short and simple. Anecdotes and jokes, provided they are brief and relevant, can add greatly to impact. Avoid mannerisms, 'ums' and 'ers' and 'you knows'.

10. Use correct technical terms, and be sure that they are understood by the class.

11. Questions are invaluable. It must be a two-way traffic for maximum class involvement. Ask the occasional thought-provoking question, then pause a moment for everyone to think it out before naming a person to answer.

Always allow time at the end to answer questions, which may often be put back to the class. If all answers are vague on a particular point, it would seem to indicate a weakness in the teaching, and clarification must be given.

If you cannot instantly recall the answer to any question, either throw it open, which may jog your memory, or suggest that the whole group research the question and compare notes next time. If you really don't know the answer, say so, and be sure to check it out before the next rally.

The five-minute talk can be invaluable to draw the ride's attention to anything of interest and from which they could learn at a rally, e.g., a loose shoe, a lame pony, any unfamiliar tack, an outstandingly good sample of hay.

The talk may be used to introduce a subject that you will enlarge on later, and which the ride could be asked to read up in their manuals. And it is ideal for a rest period in a ride, especially for juniors to discuss, for example, points of the pony, colours and markings. Riders should be dismounted to rest the ponies.

Quizzes are very popular and are a valuable incentive to learning. They might be inter-club or inter-branch contests, and the senior member of the team could be made responsible for training, with assistance from an instructor.

Smaller quizzes within a ride can be useful when revising for tests. It is still preferable to work on a team basis. Each member could be asked to prepare two questions to ask the other team — anyone who can't answer their own question loses two points for their team.

Discussion is absolutely essential for older members training new horses or preparing for advanced tests and competitions, and important for all as knowledge increases.

VISUAL AIDS

Props are essential for clear teaching. They can be handled as well as seen, and must be clean and good of their kind, unless being used intentionally to show faults.

Feed samples should be as large as possible — ideally shown in the bin in which they are stored, so that pupils can smell, feel and taste them. Failing this, a two-litre container (just on ½ gallon) holds about the minimum quantity. Small jars or plastic bags where the samples can only be seen are of little value when assessing quality. Good and bad should be included for all but very junior classes, who are learning only identification.

Hay is best shown by slices from different bales, laid out on separate sacks to avoid mixing them up. Pupils should again be encouraged to smell, feel, taste and compare.

Bits, shoes, a hoof, bones of the lower leg, preferably wired together, a horse's skull, samples of worms and bots are all valuable teaching aids.

Model jumps, both show and cross-country types, are excellent for teaching fence and course building. The 'poles' should be at least 15cm (6in) in length or they will be too difficult to see except with very small classes.

Posters and charts showing breeds of horses and ponies, points of the horse, seats of ailments, worm cycles, saddlery, etc., can be obtained from several commercial firms and displayed in the clubroom, where they make useful teaching aids. Members could be encouraged to produce their own charts.

Instructors with an artistic bent may be able to produce posters and drawings to illustrate their talks. Humorous sketches help to liven up a serious subject, especially for younger members. It is best to use large, simple line drawings — too much detail is confusing when seen from a distance.

Graphs are more suited to senior classes. Can be very useful when teaching some aspects of feeding and nutrition, for example.

Blackboard and chalk may be used to write up headings that you will develop in your talk, or to write unfamiliar words or phrases.

Writing legibly or drawing on a blackboard is not easy for the unpractised — best to do it beforehand if possible. If you want to bring out points one by one, write on the board in pencil — you will be able to see it at close quarters and go over it in chalk.

Beware, with any of the above, of standing in front of the board or picture, or of turning your back on the class. A long pointer is a great help in avoiding this.

A blackboard set up beside the school or jumping course can be useful to illustrate points during a practical lesson.

ELECTRONIC AIDS

Video, wisely used, is a most valuable teaching aid, both for viewing ready-made material and for making one's own films.

Pony Club Associations and Horse Societies have video tapes and films, which may be hired. Other instructional and general interest tapes are available from commercial firms, hire sources and embassies.

Always preview any tape you wish to use for instruction:

1. To make sure the material in it is in accordance with Pony Club principles and methods.

2. To decide exactly how much to use. Don't show too much at one time — 20 minutes would be ample for juniors to take in. Make a note of the counter settings for the sections you require. Make full use of slow motion and the occasional static picture to allow details to be absorbed. Best with small groups of similar age and standard.

As with all electronic equipment, be sure that you or your assistant know exactly how to operate it.

An evening video show with a suitably varied programme can be fun, useful for fund-raising and promoting interest, but not usually of great value from an instructional viewpoint.

Video filming requires a skilled operator with suitable equipment. The instructor should explain the objectives to both class and operator. Points to bear in mind include:

1. Every member of the ride should be filmed individually. Whether on the flat or jumping, side and either front or rear views should be taken.

2. A commentary should be an integral part of the film. The instructor can either stand close to the recorder, so that all his remarks will be picked up, add them later or comment as the film is shown.

3. Really bad pictures and unfortunate incidents should not be shown in public.

4. For junior rides, filming at the beginning and end of a lesson, so that they can see the improvement straight away, probably has the greatest impact.

More advanced riders may benefit from filming two or three times in a season, when the instructor feels that satisfactory progress can be shown. Improvement that can be seen by the rider provides the greatest possible incentive.

5. The film, with commentary, should be shown to riders as soon as possible, in the presence of the instructor.

Despite the ultimate value of video, some older members can be quite shattered at first to find that the video image falls far short of the mental image they have of themselves and their horses. Great tact may be called for — be sure to point out the good aspects. Be especially careful of making a film shortly before a test or competition, when there is not enough time to correct the faults shown.

Advanced riders should be encouraged to discuss the strengths and weaknesses in their own and each other's performances and the degree of achievement that is being attained. This is invaluable training for B and A Certificates, helping riders to assess work objectively.

Younger children are generally so excited at seeing themselves, their ponies and their friends on the screen that they are less sensitive to faults, but once they settle down watching the film should be a constructive experience for them, too.

An overhead projector is another useful aid, sometimes available from schools. Simple drawings, perhaps traced from those in the manuals, can be made on acetate with an ink pen. By superimposing these images, a picture can be built up to illustrate many points in riding and horse care.

THE WORKING RALLY

Working rallies usually include:

Riding and jumping instruction, consisting of:
1. Planning and preparation beforehand.
2. Inspection at the beginning of the rally.
3. Working in — horse and rider.
4. General work — revision or consolidation of previous lessons.
5. The 'lesson of the day' — a new subject or follow-up.
6. Summary and wind-down before proceeding to the next activity.

Unmounted instruction consisting of:
1. Checking the care of the pony during the rally.
2. A lesson on horse/pony management.
3. Visiting speakers, videos, etc.

Games, which should be incorporated into the instruction for juniors. Most members up to about C level enjoy a games period, which should be planned to suit their age and ability. Older riders may prefer a team game such as polocrosse.

Other activities could include rides out, road safety training, pace work, practice for competitions.

PLANNING AND PREPARATION

Find out beforehand:
1. The standard, age group and approximate number in the ride.
2. What is to be taught — in accordance with the overall instructional plan for this ride.
3. The time allotted for each section — flat work, jumping, etc. It is specially important to know this, and to adhere to it, when sharing equipment.
4. The space and equipment available to you.

Plan your programme so that there is a balance of physical and mental effort and relaxation. There must be interest and involvement of every member of the ride in all phases, some challenge and excitement, achievement, understanding and enjoyment throughout. All paces should be included at some stage. If your lesson of the day covers a new subject that will only involve walk, or possibly trot, include some canter in the activities before or afterwards.

Having planned each phase, decide how long you intend to spend on it. Always wear a watch to check that you are keeping reasonably well to time. Remember that it is all too easy to get bogged down in too much talk, which may become intensely boring to your ride and can disrupt the best-designed programme.

Have a back-up plan in case of unexpected changes.

On the day arrive half an hour before the start of your ride. Ensure that any equipment or props (e.g., school, jumps, bending poles) are set up or placed ready for use. If you are going to instruct mounted, allow time to work your horse in.

Meet your ride and introduce yourself. Be sure they know how to address you. Take the roll call.

It is of the utmost importance for instructors to acquire the knack of matching names to people quickly. Go over the names again — first names only — and write them down on the back of your card with any distinguishing features of pony or rider that will help you to remember them, e.g., Mary, small bay, blaze; Janet, pigtails;

John, cobby chestnut. Learning names is a skill that develops with concentration and practice.

INSPECTION

All mounted activities must begin with inspection. The primary objects are to ensure the safety, comfort and well-being of both pony and rider. It should be done by the ride instructor, whose responsibility it is.

For a working rally, clean and practical working (not show) turnout is required. For instance, the pony need not be plaited, but the mane and tail must be well brushed and tidy. Except for very junior riders, all work on the pony and tack must be the rider's own. Even the youngest should be able to show you some part that they have done themselves.

Explain the purpose of inspection. Never give the impression that any member's pony or tack are, in some way, not good enough.

In order to be quick but thorough when inspecting, try to establish a regular system. For example:

Pony and Tack	Check points
Bridle	Soundness of stitching. Holes, keepers, runners. Cheekpieces level, fitting of browband, throatlash, noseband.
Bit	Right way up, correct size, height, curb chain, if any, correctly fitted.
Reins	Correct length — often too long on small ponies. See page 66. Central buckle.
Pony's head	Well brushed, especially around ears. Eyes, nose, lips sponged. Bit injuries.
Girth area, between forelegs, under belly	Dried mud or sweat, liable to cause galls. Actual galls.
Forelegs	Obvious injuries. If any, examine and inquire further. Boots, bandages, if used, correctly fitted/applied.
Shoes/feet	Cast, loose shoes, risen clenches, long toes — lift foot, investigate further. Feet should have been picked out and be clean, conditions permitting.
Neckstrap	Fitting as for martingale neckstrap.
Martingale	Correct fitting. Rubber 'stop', rein stops.
Saddle	Fitting pony and rider. Central seat, straight on back. No weight on any part of spine, sufficient clearance at withers.

Numnah/saddle blanket	Pushed up into front arch. No rucks or wrinkles, especially under saddle flaps. Weight should not come on a fold.
Girth	Correct length for pony, soft, sound. Buckles and stitching.
Girth straps	Soundness, holes, buckle guards. When inspecting these, rider must put leg over front of flap, keeping foot in stirrup.
Stirrup-irons	Correct size and type. Treads fitting.
Stirrup leathers	Stitching, holes, overall soundness, level.
Pony's hindquarters	Cleanliness, especially tail and dock.
Hind legs, as forelegs	
Rider	*Check points*
Headgear	Approved type, well fitting, sound and correctly worn. Tidy hair. Warn against earrings.
Footwear	Safe, suitable type, clean.
Pony Club uniform	As required by club. Clean and tidy. Badge, with test felt or clip. Whip and spurs, see pages 84–85.

Check the pony's condition, and the cleanliness of pony and tack, according to the standard of the ride.

While inspecting, check again on each rider's name. Ask, if you don't already know, the pony's name and age and the rider's interests, problems, and ambitions. Give generous praise to good turnout, especially any improvement, or obvious results from lessons on grooming, tack cleaning, etc.

This may look a formidable list, but with regular attenders who are known to the instructor, with practice and strict adherence to a system, it should not take much more than about a minute per rider. Major problems should be sorted out at the beginning of the season.

Long-winded, 'nit-picking' inspections are time-consuming and very off-putting, especially for boys. Be brisk but thorough.

A large ride of unknown newcomers will take much longer initially. It will save time to have one or more well-briefed assistants to carry out any necessary alterations. (Check again yourself before starting the ride.) A leather punch, spare numnahs, wither pads, neckstraps, etc., could be useful to have on hand.

Ponies must not be ridden if:
1. Seriously lame. Older ponies are sometimes rather stiff and rheu-

matic when starting work and may loosen up after a few minutes, any pony can hit himself and go 'sore' for a short time, but no pony may be ridden with a persistent or severe lameness.

2. They have any injury likely to cause pain or lameness if worked.
3. They have a cough or a runny nose, unless the cough is certified by the vet to be non-infectious. Otherwise, the pony must be removed at once from the rally and kept in isolation until recovered.
4. In very poor condition, obviously exhausted or out of sorts, or showing signs of colic. Mares heavy in foal.
5. In urgent need of shoeing, affecting their action.
6. The rider has no suitable headgear.

Ponies may be ridden bareback only if:
1. The saddle comes down, and cannot be padded up sufficiently to keep it clear of withers or spine.
2. The girth or girth straps are dangerous, or the girth is too long.
3. The pony has bad girth galls.

Stirrups must not be used if they are dangerously large or small for the rider or the stirrup leathers are unsafe.

It is naturally disappointing for a child to be unable to ride their pony at a rally, but we must never lose sight of one of the most important objects of Pony Club — 'to instil into members the proper care of their animals'. Of course, one should be sympathetic and try to suggest ways to help the pony, but instructors must be quite clear and firm on this point. 'Your pony is your friend and your responsibility, and you must not expect him to work for you if he is not feeling well.'

Try to keep the rider involved, watching, helping, and possibly having a short ride on another member's pony, by invitation.

If a pony is dangerous to its rider or to others, is totally unsuitable or unfit, consult the Head or Chief Instructor or District Commissioner, then, if necessary, discuss the problem in their presence with the parents. Clubs should take all possible steps to encourage inexperienced parents to seek advice before buying either pony or tack.

Be wary of sending parents verbal messages, which tend to get misinterpreted or forgotten. Try to speak to the parents personally.

Whips
Once a rider can hold and handle the reins correctly, a whip should always be carried, except where it is forbidden, as in gymkhana games and some dressage tests.

The purpose of the whip is to draw attention to the leg aids, to back up or clarify them — rarely for punishment. Riders must be taught how to carry a whip in either hand, to change it from one hand to the other, and to use it correctly.

Several types of whip are shown in *Manual No 2*, page 32. No 1 is good for D and C riders, for those on young horses, and for everybody for jumping. Loops, as in No 2, should be removed. They can be dangerous in the event of a fall, and inhibit the proper use of the whip.

Dressage whips should not be used by riders below C level, and never, by anybody, for jumping or for punishment. The cane is correct in the show ring, but unsuitable for everyday riding and training.

Spurs

A good type of spur, correctly fitted, is shown in *Manual No 2*, page 33.

Spurs must not be used by beginners. Riders must first establish a steady position and learn to use their legs correctly, assisted by the whip if need be. In exceptional circumstances, such as a small but steady rider on a large, leg-proof pony, permission may be given to use spurs.

Spurs should never be used on a horse who does not understand the basic leg aids.

It should be understood that spurs are a refinement, and that they are not normally necessary or desirable for work below B standard. The practice of using them indiscriminately, at any level, should be actively discouraged.

TAKING RIDES ON THE FLAT

1. Working-in, preferably in the open, as explained on page 38. Start at walk on a long rein, if possible, followed by a few minutes in rising trot on both reins, to get ponies and riders loosened up and settled. Canter should only be included at this stage with rides of C level or beyond. Observe good and bad points, but make only urgent corrections and keep comments to a minimum.

Bring the ride in and line them up. Check stirrup lengths where necessary, praise good points and tell each rider briefly what they should concentrate on to improve themselves and their ponies.

Continue with a few minutes' work on the rider's position. This could include physical exercises, sitting trot, with or without stirrups.

2. Revision or consolidation of a previous lesson in a different form, or exercises in preparation for the next phase. Ways must be found to incorporate the large amount of revision and repetition that is necessary, without the instruction becoming monotonous.

3. The lesson of the day. See page 37. Would usually be brought in about 15 to 20 minutes after the start of the ride, and would last from 15 to 30 minutes, depending on the complexity of the subject, the number in the ride and their age, ability and attention span.

4. Some 'wind-down' activity will ensure finishing on a good note. It could be a game or an exercise that the ride enjoys doing and does well.

JUMPING RIDES

1. Most of the exercises on the large circle (see page 40) are useful when working rides in for jumping. Stirrups will be shortened, riders in jumping position, and full attention should be paid to this and to the horses' balance, paces, bend, correct canter leads, etc. Transitions, working halts and lengthening and shortening of stride are of particular value. Rides that have been working on the flat before jumping, will require a shorter period of working in.

Make use of trotting poles and/or cavalleti — see page 67.

Jumping a few small fences at trot in single file, with the ride about six lengths apart, gets everybody warmed up and going freely, without the undue excitement that might develop in canter. See *Manual No 2*, page 68.

2. Work on position, contact, approach, etc. Jumping a single fence, individually. Each rider may have several turns. Where there are faults, the instructor must explain, and if necessary, demonstrate, where improvement is needed, before the next attempt.

The ride should be lined up facing the jump, watching and commenting when asked. While one rider is jumping, the next should be out, circling near the fence in readiness.

In cold weather, especially with large rides, the whole ride may walk or trot on a large circle in open order round the fence, each member turning in and jumping when called by name by the instructor. Each rider can still have several attempts.

3. The lesson of the day, e.g., jumping without reins, gymnastic exercises, riding a course, combinations, up/downhill, ditches etc.

4. It is usually preferable that the ride should dismount, run up stirrups, slacken girths and lead their ponies away at the end of a jumping session.

INST

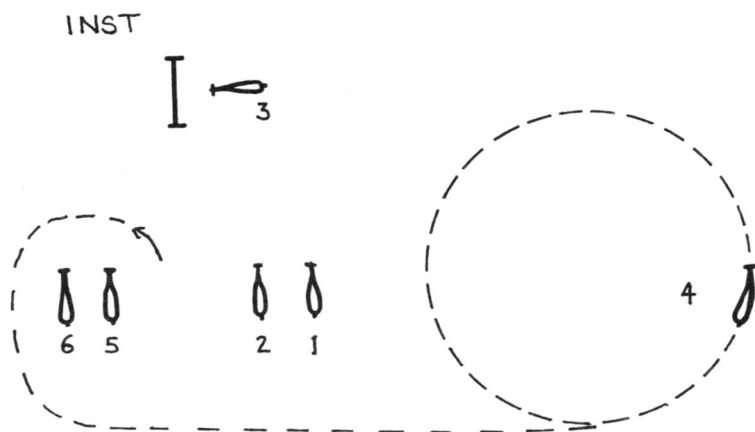

A jumping lesson over a single fence. Nos 1 and 2 have had their turns, No 3 is approaching the fence, No 4, circling, with the pony balanced and on the correct leg, ready to jump when called. No 5 will then take No 4's place on the circle.

At every rally try to include at least one new fact or piece of information, however minor. It could take the form of a five-minute talk (see page 77), and can make a useful break after a period of energetic physical activity.

3
TEACHING YOUNG BEGINNERS & RIDERS UP TO D CERTIFICATE

Where it all begins. No Pony Club uniform as yet, but the right sturdy and independent attitude.

Standard. Very basic, riding and pony care. Foundations of position, aids, ability to control the pony reasonably well in the paddock or 'out and about' accompanied by older riders. Early stages of learning about the pony and how to handle it. Needs constant supervision.

CRITERIA FOR INSTRUCTORS

D/C course with National Instructor, if possible, or a basic course conducted or arranged by the Chief/Head Instructor.

Sound knowledge of *Manual No 1* and of C work generally, to see where the instruction is leading. Detailed knowledge of the D section. Apart from this, deep technical knowledge is not essential.

Some experience as a leading file/demonstrator/assistant before taking rides on their own.

Enthusiasm, and the special ability to communicate with younger children — a gift which not everybody possesses.

INSTRUCTOR'S OBJECTIVES

1. Familiarisation. To help the rider to get to know the pony and feel at home with it. To develop confidence at walk and trot, with the pony led at first, if necessary.

2. Technique. To develop balance and co-ordination, by means of exercises, short periods of work on position, changes of pace and direction, and games. Mount and dismount, rising trot, handling the reins. Towards the end of this stage start canter, walk/trot over scattered poles.

3. Control. Concept of very simple aids for controlling the pony in transitions and turns.

4. Pony Care. To teach the basics of approaching, handling and caring for the pony safely, sensibly and sympathetically.

Problems

Unsuitable ponies and gear, sometimes dangerous and often bought without prior consultation.

Uninterested parents, some of whom feel they have done enough by supplying pony and gear, and are unwilling to learn sufficient for adequate supervision. More rarely at this stage, over-enthusiastic parents who push too hard.

Sometimes a family lack of animal sense and experience.

TAKING D RIDES

With complete beginners an enclosure is essential — a small paddock, fenced-off corner of a larger one, well-roped school or all-weather arena.

Riders unable to cope must have someone to lead and assist. Preferably a parent who can attend the lesson, so that practice at home can continue on recommended lines. Draw the attention of parents to *Manual No 1*, Chapters 1, 2 and 3.

Points to remember:

While children of this age are extremely keen to learn, many have no experience with animals of any kind, so tend to be either nervous or insensitive in their dealings with them. Few have any built-in animal sense. This calls for constant vigilance on the part of the instructor.

Natural balance and suppleness vary tremendously. Many youngsters are surprisingly stiff and unco-ordinated, especially when they are tense, nervous or excited — as they may well be when they first come to Pony Club.

This age-group has a very limited 'attention span', therefore 10 to 15 minutes is the maximum period for instruction without a break. Alternate instruction with games to practise points in the lesson, and with short talks.

Special checks at inspection: See page 82.

Soundness and fitting of all tack.

Size of stirrup-irons, especially if a pad saddle without safety bars is used.

Length of reins — tie a knot in them if they are long enough to catch round the rider's foot. See page 66.

Neckstraps.

Pony's health and well-being — condition, feet, mouth, back, girth. Check-cord may be needed to prevent grazing. See *Manual No 1*, page 116.

POSITION

Reference: *Manual No 1*, pages 22–25.

Stirrups fairly short. Always check that they are level, and check the rider's straightness.

Work on one or two things at a time — e.g., head up, heels down — and gradually build up the picture.

Constant attention is needed to holding the reins correctly. For evenness and correct length, it can help to put an elastic band on each rein. Rein drill — i.e., picking up, shortening, lengthening, putting both reins into either hand — should be practised from the first lesson. *Note:* It is best with very small hands to have the little finger inside the rein.

Exercises should also be included from the first lesson. Initially at the halt, keeping the stirrups, then without stirrups, at halt and walk. Cross stirrups, right one first, on the pony's shoulders, not on the saddle. Pulling the buckle slightly down from the safety bar may facilitate this.

There are two types of exercises, position and agility:

Position exercises — the leg position must be maintained, whatever the upper part of the body is doing. Examples: body bending forward, toe touching, airplane exercise, arm circling. Check positions between each exercise.

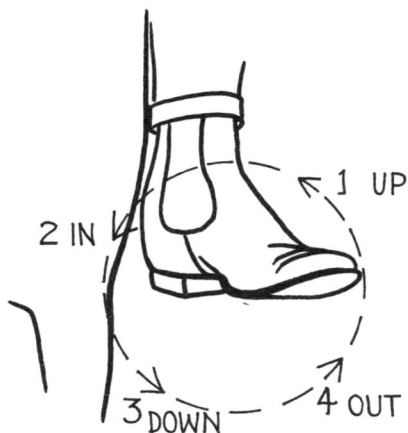

Ankle-turning. Toe up, in, down, out. Foot may be rotated in both directions.

Agility exercises — for balance, suppleness, confidence. Examples: leg-swinging, ankle-turning, 'round the world', heel clicking. Ponies must be held during exercises, at least until the ponies are known to be quiet, and always for 'round the world', etc. See *Manual No 1*, pages 29–30.

AIDS

Reference: *Manual No 1*, pages 26–29.

Legs. Avoid the word 'squeeze' — 'close' the legs to attract the pony's attention or in downward transitions. 'Tap' or 'nudge' for upward transitions. Leg aids are given 'at' (i.e., just behind) the girth, with the inside of the calf, and with the heels down.

Hands. Always check length and evenness of reins before transitions or turns. Note use of hands to 'Walk on', while walking and coming to halt. Learning to follow the movement of the pony's head and neck at walk is the first step towards a feeling contact.

Back and seat. No mention at this stage, other than 'Sit tall'. It may help to take a deep breath in to achieve this, but be sure the child lets the breath out again.

Watch correct order of the aids — 'Sit tall' and use of legs always precede hands.

Voice. Emphasise this — it is most important in developing feeling and understanding for the pony as a partner. Many ponies will obey the other aids more easily in conjunction with a 'Walk on' or 'Steady', but the 'Good boy (or girl)' the moment the pony does obey is the essential thing. Point out how much ponies like quiet praise and encouragement with the voice, how confused they become with loud screams and shouting.

Turning aids. 'Open' inside rein — check that the hand comes away from the pony's neck, over the rider's knee, keeping the thumb on top. There must be no backward tension. Practising the positioning of hands and legs at halt, without actually applying the aids is an excellent exercise in understanding and co-ordination.

SUITABLE SCHOOL EXERCISES

In single file: Change of rein on the diagonal. Turns down the centre and across the school. Transitions. See page 45.

In succession: Trot front to rear. Halting from the rear. Leading files up and down the centre. See page 49.

In rides: Turns across the school. As above, with change of direction. See page 55.

TEACHING TROT

Reference: *Manual No 1*, page 28.

The first objective is to get the rider doing a reasonable trot, sitting quietly (not rising) in a correct position, holding the saddle, not neckstrap, to maintain balance. Practise lots of short, slow trots. It may be necessary to have the pony led at this stage.

SPECIMEN LESSONS

Rising trot

Explain that there are two ways of riding at the trot — sitting, as we have been doing, and rising. Sitting gives more control and you can use your aids more clearly, but rising is easier for pony and rider for long periods of trot. Leader demonstrates during explanation, emphasising that you always sit for the first and last few strides of trot. Point out the pony's two-time action at trot, and how the rider goes forward, not up, and down in time with the pony's step, keeping the hands down and very steady. Do not mention diagonals, but the demonstrator should use them correctly.

Practise the 'rising' action at halt, making sure that the lower leg remains in place. Point out how this affects your balance — if the lower leg is too far forward you can't rise at all, if too far back you will flop forward over the pony's neck.

Trot on from walk, sitting until all are settled, then rising for a short distance. Back to walk, emphasising sit down on 'Prepare to walk'. Repeat several times.

Show any faults that occurred, followed by the correct way, then work on individual improvement.

Common faults:

Rising out of time with the pony. Most children will soon get the rhythm with practice. In case of difficulty, take the child alone for a few minutes and count the beat of the pony's trot, one, two, one, two, changing to up, down, up, down, then get the child to take over the counting. Most people rise too slowly at first.

Rising too high, and/or pushing up instead of letting the pony's action do the work. Both these faults can come from trying too hard, and very often from being behind the pony's movement. The lower leg may be too far forward.

Rising trot, correct. Body a little forward — note direction of 'rise'.

Rising trot, incorrect. Rider 'pushing up' out of stirrups.

Hands 'rising' with the body. Keep the little fingers touching the top of the pony's shoulders until the problem is overcome, but watch that this doesn't lead to pushing up with the hands.

Finish with questions: How many ways of riding at the trot? What are they? Why do we sit/rise? Pony's action at trot? Where should head, heels, lower leg, hands be when rising?

Comment upon individual faults, what to work on at home.

First canter

Reference: *Manual No 1*, pages 31–32.

Prerequisite: All must be capable of rising trot, and have control on walk-trot transitions.

It is suggested that, if the ponies are suitably quiet for beginners, this lesson should be given on a large circle in a not-too-large enclosure, cantering from front to rear of the ride. This will be easier for the riders than cantering round the corners of the school. It may be helpful to trot front to rear first, so that the ponies know what is coming and that they are going to fit in behind.

Emphasise the importance of steadying in time at the end of the exercise.

Use leader to demonstrate canter, including basic aids from trot to canter and back again. The pony should be on the correct leg, but don't talk about this yet. The first object is for riders to get the feel of the pony moving at canter. Point out the 'rocking horse' movement, and how still the rider can sit without being stiff. As always, head up, heels and hands down. If the rider feels at all unsteady, he puts a hand on the pommel of the saddle or neckstrap.

Canter front to rear, each cantering only a short distance, then back through trot to fit in behind at walk.

Demonstrate any faults that occurred, followed by the correct way, and repeat. Provided the ponies were calm and under control the first time, the second canter may be longer.

Common faults:

'Bumping' or losing balance, usually caused by: stiffness, hands too high, tension, holding breath or gripping too tightly. Tell the rider to hold the pommel, keep the bend in the knee. Ask a simple question (rider will have to draw breath while answering!).

Ponies that trot faster and faster instead of cantering: bring back at once to steady pace. Emphasise that the rider must make the leg aids very clear, while sitting still and keeping sufficient rein contact to prevent the pony from going faster. Legs first tell the pony to canter, then hands let him do it. It can help to send the pony two or three lengths behind another, quiet pony, which will canter freely. In extreme cases, try sending the pony out away from the ride about 50m, to turn round a marker and return at canter. Doing this too frequently would lead to nappiness, but it is usually effective in getting the pony going so that the rider can get the feel of canter.

The leading leg is not important at this stage. If the exercise is done on the left rein most ponies will probably lead correctly. If they do not, it will not matter as much on the big circle as it would round corners in the school.

Finish with questions on position, aids, etc.

WALK ON LONG REIN

Of great importance at this level. The rider gains confidence from the realisation that the pony will not 'take off' if he is given rein. Explain that his neck and back muscles get tired when he has been working, so he must often be allowed to have a good stretch to loosen them up.

For the pony, this relief from the inevitable unsteadiness of the beginner's hands is necessary for his well-being and continued good temper. See illustration in *Manual No 1*, page 64.

The method of lengthening and shortening the reins will be taught during rein drill. It is preferable, both for safety and for developing the rider's feel, that the pony should be 'offered' and allowed to take as much rein as he requires, rather than dropping the reins on to the buckle.

POLES ON THE GROUND

Walking, and later trotting, over scattered poles is an invaluable exercise for the D level rider. Even pretending to jump gives great satisfaction, and provides a real incentive in learning to guide and control the pony.

Emphasise from the beginning (and demonstrate) — aim at right angles to the centre of each pole, go straight, before, over and after. Rider looks up towards the next pole, pony looks down at the one he is stepping over. The hands must follow forward and down to let him do this. See *Manual No 1*, page 78.

GAMES

The following games are good fun, and excellent for putting into practice all that has been taught in the instructional sessions.

For transitions
Grandmother's footsteps, or creeping up
Requirements: none (except a courageous instructor).
The ride is lined up at one end of the school or other enclosure. The instructor stands at the opposite end, facing outwards. On the word 'Go' the ride tries to 'creep up' on the instructor, who turns at intervals to look back. Anyone seen to be moving returns to the base line. To avoid ponies' mouths being pulled about, it is advisable to count to three, out loud, before turning round.

For mounting and dismounting, leading in hand
Musical sacks
Requirements: markers, tyres or cones, not stakes, on a large circle. Sacks, one less than the number of participants, placed on a fairly small circle inside the markers. Music, or failing this, a whistle.

The ride trots or canters (specify the pace, according to ability) outside the markers. When the music stops or the whistle sounds, they dismount, run up stirrups, put reins over pony's head and run to the nearest sack. Continue, removing one more sack each time. When it comes to the last two riders, they should go round in opposite directions.

This method, dismounting outside the markers, is safer with inexperienced riders as it avoids collisions in the centre.

This game may also be played as 'musical people', with people replacing the sacks. This ensures assistance with re-mounting, where needed. (Holding ponies, not legging up.)
Walk, trot and lead race
Requirements: two markers, at each end of the course. A steward will be needed at the other end from the instructor.

The ride is lined up at one end, walks down the school, trots back, then dismounts, runs up stirrups, reins over pony's head, and leads to the other end. If all are capable, they remount, the winner being the first one to finish mounted, with feet correctly in stirrups.

If a pony breaks, it must be turned on a complete circle (gently).
Stepping-stone race
Requirements: solid firewood rounds (not concrete blocks), set at a distance to suit. Markers for start and finish. See illustration in *Manual No 1*, page 95.

Start with teams mounted behind markers. Each in turn rides to the first stepping-stone, dismounts and runs over stepping-stones, leading the pony, to the far end, remounts and rides back to the start.

For turning and guiding the pony

Bending at walk and trot

Requirements: two or three sets of six bending poles, 9m (30ft) apart.

This will not be a race at this stage, but the ride should be divided into teams and points given for the smoothest performances. When all are capable of riding with reins in one hand, a baton could be carried and passed, behind the base line, to the next member of the team.

Riding the maze

Requirements: poles and markers to lay out a 'track' to be followed.

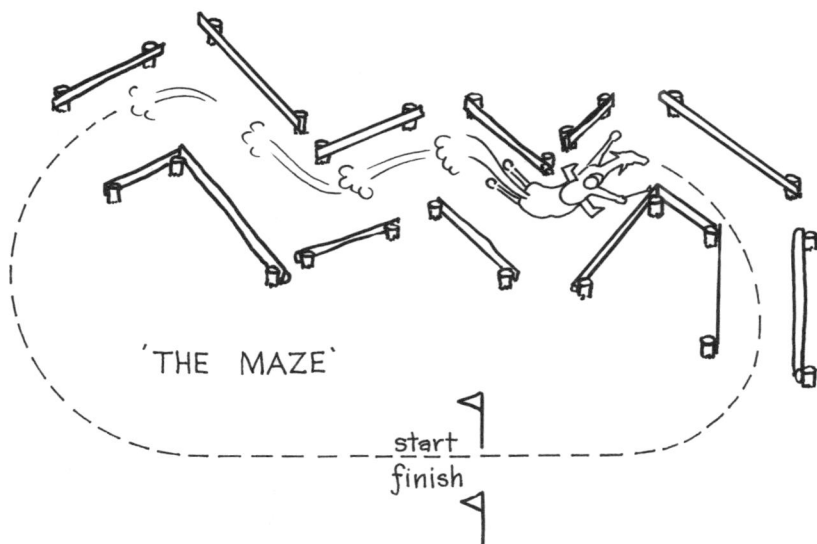

Riding the 'maze'.

For riding with reins in one hand

The handkerchief game

Requirement: a large handkerchief or small scarf. Best conducted in a dressage arena or other fairly small enclosure.

This game is the essence of simplicity, but young children love it. For them, the pace should be limited to trot.

One rider is given the handkerchief at the start, and everyone else tries to snatch it. It must not be raised above shoulder height or crossed over the pony's spine, and must be relinquished when somebody else has a firm grip on it. Anyone who takes their reins in both hands or canters with the handkerchief must forfeit it to the nearest person.

Check that the reins are held correctly in one hand, and change to the other hand at 'half-time'. Make sure that everybody has a turn.

Any form of flag or relay race that involves carrying something on the pony will give practice in the important skill of riding with the reins in one hand.

For general alertness and observation
Do this! Do that!
Requirements: none.
Excellent for practising exercises, either at halt or walking round the instructor on a circle, with or without stirrups. The instructor performs various actions or exercises. When he says 'Do this!' the ride does it, but if he says 'Do That!' they don't. Commands must be given quite quickly. Anybody doing the wrong thing loses a 'life'. Check at the end who has lost the least 'lives'.
Follow my leader
Can be tremendous fun and very educational with an imaginative and safety-conscious leader.

For general control of the pony
Scavenger hunt
Requirements: mounting blocks and stewards to assist as needed.
There are numerous variations on the scavenger hunt. The following are good ones for D Certificate riders who can control their ponies in the open paddock. Limit the pace to walk or trot, if necessary.
1. Scatter a variety of articles around in a given area — e.g., a matchbox, shoelace, ball, etc. They may be placed on fence posts, in branches, etc., so that most can be collected without dismounting.

Allow a set time. The winner is the person who brings the largest number of articles, which must be delivered all together, not singly.
2. Prepare a list of six to ten articles you know can be found in the paddock — you may have to 'plant' some of them. It could include specific leaves, flowers or grasses, something a bird might use in building its nest — whatever your imagination suggests.

Assemble the ride, show samples of any items on the list that may be unfamiliar to them, then send them off to find the first one. Some of the items, but not all, should necessitate dismounting, but each must be delivered with the rider mounted. As each rider brings items to you, tell them the next one to look for, and so on. The winner is, of course, the person who first delivers all the items on your list.

If the club ground is large or there are quiet roads nearby, these young riders could be paired with older members to search for articles over a wider area. The older member would be given the complete list and perhaps a sack or knapsack, and a time limit set.

These games are useful for mixing the age-groups, and encouraging a sense of responsibility among the seniors.

The message game

Requirements: none.

The ride is evenly spaced out round the perimeter of a large paddock, except for No 1, who is given a message by the instructor in the centre of the paddock (e.g., 'Please send a bag of pony pellets and a sack of chaff at once. All the ponies are hungry!'). No 1 then rides to No 2, delivers the message, and remains in No 2's place. No 2 rides on to No 3, and so on through the ride. The message must only be given once to each person. The last one returns to the instructor with the final version. He then rides round, picking up all messengers en route, who return to discuss how the message came to them.

Good for teaching riders to make their ponies go away from one another, and stand quietly on their own. Could be done with almost complete beginners if energetic pony-leaders are available.

FIVE-MINUTE TALK SUBJECTS

Describing own pony, colour, sex, markings.

Points of the pony. One or two at a time, with something about each, e.g., withers, highest point of the pony's spine when his head is low, therefore this is where he is measured. Very sensitive — there must never be any weight or pressure on the withers.

Knee — corresponds to your wrist, has same bones.

Hock — your heel.

Hoof — the pony's middle finger or toe — imagine running on two fingers and two toes!

The pony's mouth — show incisors, bars of mouth — feel sharpness of jawbone — imagine effects of rough hands and steel bit.

Emphasise correct approach and handling when indicating points.

The pony's mind — very simply.

Parts of bridle, bit, saddle, girth, stirrup-irons and leathers.

CARE OF THE PONY

Teaching at this level will depend to some extent on the rider's age. Younger members, as well as being shown correct methods, will need encouragement and actual, physical help to carry them out, particularly if they have a big pony. Requirements are really basic — e.g., brushing the pony over, rather than full-scale grooming. While keeping it simple, it is still essential that all details should be taught and correct habits formed. Aim to develop safe practices and a sense of responsibility for the pony's well-being.

SPECIMEN LESSON

Approaching and handling, tying-up, giving a titbit
Reference: *Manual No 1*, pages 35–37.
Requirements: A quiet pony, suitable size, halter, two lead-ropes, tying rail, binder twine, carrots (cut lengthways) as titbits.

Explain that ponies are nervous creatures, especially scary of things approaching from behind, or of sudden movements. With somebody holding the pony, show how to approach and handle it, and use of voice.

Demonstrate: how and where to tie a pony up safely — use of binder twine and quick-release knot.

Demonstrate: tying quick-release knot, using spare rope, without pony. All practise tying knot.

Demonstrate: tying the pony up, with correct length of rope, giving a titbit.

Ride in turn practise this, with own ponies, if possible.

Prove the lesson.

SIX-RALLY PROGRAMME

A rally at D level will usually include riding, pony care and games or a ride out — probably round the club grounds.
Riding sessions, 45 minutes overall maximum, will include:
Inspection, check stirrup lengths.
Work-in, walk/trot, as capable.
Check position, holding reins. Exercises and/or rein drill.
Revision, possibly including game for practice.
Lesson of the day.
Five-minute talk on riding or pony care.
Game, incorporating some aspect of what has been taught.
Sum up, suggest what to practise at home, dismount, run up stirrups, lead away.
Position and holding/handling reins are ongoing, will be taught/checked/discussed at every rally.

Lessons of the day will include:
Mounting and dismounting.
Aids for transitions.
Aids for turning.

Rising trot.
Walk on long rein.
Canter.
Walk/trot over poles on the ground.
Revision as required before D Certificate.

Pony Care, 20 minutes maximum, will include:
Approaching and handling, tying-up, giving a titbit.
Catching and turning out.
Leading in hand.
Brushing over.
Points of the pony and parts of saddlery — probably taught mainly during rest periods in rides.
Constant attention to correct approach and handling of pony.

Lessons should also be given in these periods on 'What Pony Club is all About' and 'Riding on the Road'.
Further games or ride out. 30 minutes maximum.

A six-rally plan for Ds could therefore include, after inspection and work-in:

Rally No 1
Riding: Explanation, demonstration and practice of position at halt, walk, and trot, if capable. How to hold the reins.
Simple exercises, with stirrups, rein drill.
Lesson: Aids — meaning of the word (signals) — aids for walk and halt.
Five-minute talk: Describing ponies — colour, sex, individual ponies.
Game: Grandmother's footsteps.
Pony care: Approaching and handling pony, tying-up, giving a titbit.
Game: Scavenger hunt, with unmounted assistance, as needed.

Rally No 2
Riding: Revision exercise, halting from rear.
Lesson: Aids for turning.
Five-minute talk: Markings. Dismount (run up stirrups) to see markings, remount, check method.
Game: Riding the maze.
Pony care: Catching and turning out, leading in hand.
Games: Do this! Do that! and/or Follow my leader. Ponies led if necessary.

Rally No 3
Riding: Revision exercise, turns across the school in rides, walk.

Lesson: Rising trot.
Five-minute talk: A few points of the pony — dismount, etc., as above.
Game: Walk, trot and lead race.
Pony care: The pony's needs (water, food, shelter, etc.). Very simply.
Game: Bending at walk and trot.

Rally No 4
Riding: General revision to date. No new lesson, but work on trot front to rear of the ride and introduce leaders up and down the centre at walk.
Rein drill, emphasis on putting reins into either hand.
Five-minute talk: Questions and discussion.
Game: The handkerchief game.
Pony care: Pony Club, what it's all about. Remind ride to bring brushes to next rally.
Games: Musical sacks. Carrying a flag.

Rally No 5
Riding: Revision exercise. Leaders up and down the centre, walk and trot.
Lesson: Canter.
Five-minute talk: The pony's mouth and the bit.
Pony care: Brushing the pony over. Ponies correctly tied up, on tying rail.
Games: Ride round the club ground. Message game for those capable.

Rally No 6
Revision: Turns across the school in rides at trot.
Riding: Walk/trot over poles on the ground.
Revision: Canter front to rear.
Five-minute talk: Parts of the saddle and bridle.
Game: The handkerchief game.
Pony care: Riding on the road, do's and don'ts.
Bending, canter for those capable. Flag race in teams.

SITTING D CERTIFICATE

Most members should be ready during their first season — when the record card is filled and the instructor is satisfied they can do everything required. As this test is largely for encouragement, it should not be unduly delayed, and an examiner should be available at most rallies.

4

TEACHING OLDER BEGINNERS & RIDERS UP TO C CERTIFICATE

A typical C Certificate ride.

This is the largest group at Pony Club. To quote *Manual No 1*, 'It is hoped that everyone will do their best to attain C Certificate level, to ensure that they can ride well enough to establish a safe and happy partnership with their ponies, and that all ponies are cared for to a reasonable standard.'

C standard implies that the rider's seat is becoming established, that he knows and can apply the aids for simple movements, can jump small fences without interfering with the pony's action and is forming good habits in riding and pony care. Above all, that he has control of the pony and can ride it safely and sensibly alone or in company, particularly on the road.

He should be able, with some supervision, to care for the pony in its daily life and work, recognising the signs of good and bad health and knowing when to seek adult assistance.

He should be learning something of the Pony Club movement and its traditions.

CRITERIA FOR INSTRUCTORS

C–C+ course with a National Instructor.

Thorough knowledge of, and constant reference to, *Manual No 1*. Should also be familiar with at least the B section of *Manual No 2*.

Deeper knowledge — ability to recognise good points and basic faults in rider's position, application of aids, pony's paces and way of going, and be able to praise or correct accordingly. Must be able to tell whether the rider is on the correct diagonal, the pony cantering on the proper leg, etc. Should see the picture as a whole rather than picking on minor details.

A lively and adaptable mind, to maintain interest through the inevitable repetition at this stage. Ability to keep order and insist that such things as mounting, leading, altering stirrups, etc., are carried out correctly *always*, without nagging or becoming too 'heavy'.

Practical experience of riding, and of looking after own horse, or own children's ponies.

INSTRUCTOR'S OBJECTIVES

1. Familiarisation. To develop the rider's understanding of the pony and its probable reactions, and his confidence at all paces, up and down hill as well as on the flat and over small fences.

To introduce the idea of establishing respect and confidence between pony and rider — making sure the pony understands, then insisting on obedience and praising it the moment it obeys.

2. Technique. To develop the firmness and independence of the seat on the flat, enabling the rider to apply the aids more accurately.

To establish a sound basic jumping position over trotting poles and small jumps.

3. Control. Sufficient to enable the rider to go 'out and about' with others or alone (provided the pony is traffic-proof and otherwise suitable), and to take part in all Pony Club activities for riders of their standard.

4. Pony Care. To teach members to care for their ponies and equipment, with supervision. To develop powers of observation and knowledge of the requirements for their own pony's well-being throughout the year.

Problems

Very large rides, mixed with regard to age, ability, interests and size of mounts.

Ages can range from 8 to 18 — an impossible task for an instructor to maintain interest at both ends of the scale.

Ability can vary from just post- (or even pre-) D to riders who are competing (and sometimes winning) in quite advanced competition, though sometimes without adequate foundations.

Some can see no reason to acquire such foundations. Tact and subtlety, combined with firmness at times, may be needed to convince them.

Interests — from the highly ambitious competitive rider to the many members who enjoy their ponies and the company of their peers, without ever wanting to go beyond local branch or club competitions, or to compete at all.

Mounts, ranging from small ponies to big horses, possibly including ex-racehorses, trotters and pacers, present almost insuperable problems when working on combined exercises in the school or over trotting poles or combinations. They can also vary from the 'ploddy' type to the excitable show jumper or eventer, often beyond the control of riders at this stage.

Older beginners are better in a post-D ride because:

1. Although they will be technically less competent than their classmates, their greater mental capacity and muscle control should enable them to catch up fairly quickly. The challenge should keep everybody on their toes, whereas older members in a junior ride will feel they are being 'talked down to' and will lose interest. They should be quite capable of understanding, for instance, the reasons for keeping the correct position, which will be taught at the beginning of the C work.

2. Their mounts will be too big among the small 'junior' ponies.

Care must be taken that these beginners cover all the work for D Certificate. This can be a useful revision for others in the ride, who can act as demonstrators.

Except in small branches, there will probably be several rides between D and C. The above factors should be borne in mind when dividing these rides.

Where there is only one very mixed ride and one instructor available, it would be best to divide it into two sections for riding and jumping lessons — one half receiving instruction while the others are occupied playing games and/or learning care of the pony with someone else.

For lessons in pony care, all should be interested in learning to look after their mounts — it is up to the instructor to create the enthusiasm. Riding ability and size of mount have little or no bearing, but it is still desirable to avoid a very mixed age-group.

105

TAKING PRE-C RIDES

Rider's position Reference: *Manual No 1*, pages 45–48.
Overall picture: pony and rider moving as one, in balance with one another. Rider supple, steady and quiet, especially with hand and lower leg. Suitable length of stirrup. *Manual No 1*, page 52.
Check:
1. Vertical line, ear, shoulder, hip, heel.
2. Stirrup leather vertical, *inside* of calf in contact with the pony's side.
3. Knee and toe pointing forward, heel down.
4. Straight line from elbow to bit, bent elbow, soft wrist.
5. Reins held correctly, both little fingers the same, inside or outside the rein; thumbs on top and on rein, not whip, fingers closed and spare end of rein between the reins and the pony's neck.
6. Whip lying on thigh denotes correct hand/arm position.
From behind (see *Manual No 1*, page 23):
7. Saddle straight on pony's back.
8. Rider's/pony's spines in line.

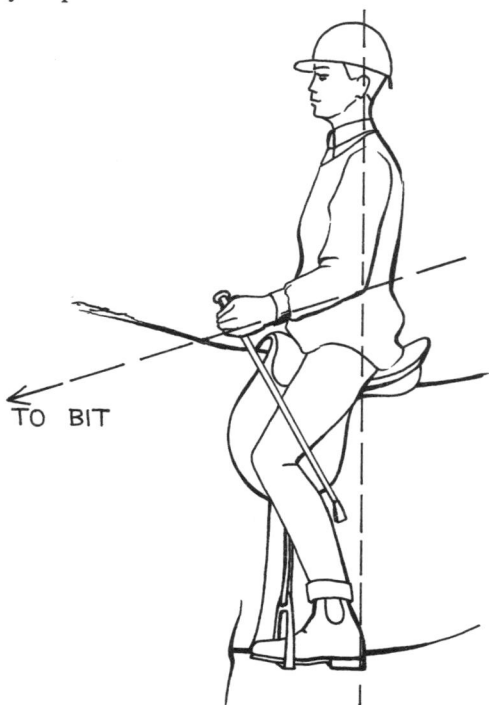

TO BIT

Check points for rider's position.

IMPROVING THE POSITION

1. Quick, regular check after work-in, emphasising good points, what has improved, what still needs improvement, what to think about during the lesson.

2. Riding without stirrups, *Manual No 1*, pages 49–50. Practise both 'position' and 'activity' exercises at halt and walk. A series of exercises to loosen up the whole body from head to heels is excellent.

At trot, note progression — hold saddle until balanced and steady, then hand on thigh or arm down to side, but hold again immediately if balance is lost. Don't attempt other arm positions or exercises too soon.

Arm circling — best forward, up, over, back and down, which straightens back and shoulders. Arm and fingers relaxed.

Occasional practice in walk, halt, walk transitions, concentrating on stretching down, not pulling up, when using leg, is very valuable.

3. Trot with stirrups — sitting, rising, standing — *Manual No 1*, pages 51–53.

Exercises: (a) Six strides sitting (12 beats), six strides rising, alternately, trying to maintain the same rhythm throughout.

(b) Sitting, holding saddle, rising, hand on thigh, standing, hand resting on mane at first, then hand on hip, maintaining rhythm as above. *Note:* Standing trot is excellent for leg position and balance, especially for rides of Pre-C3 level.

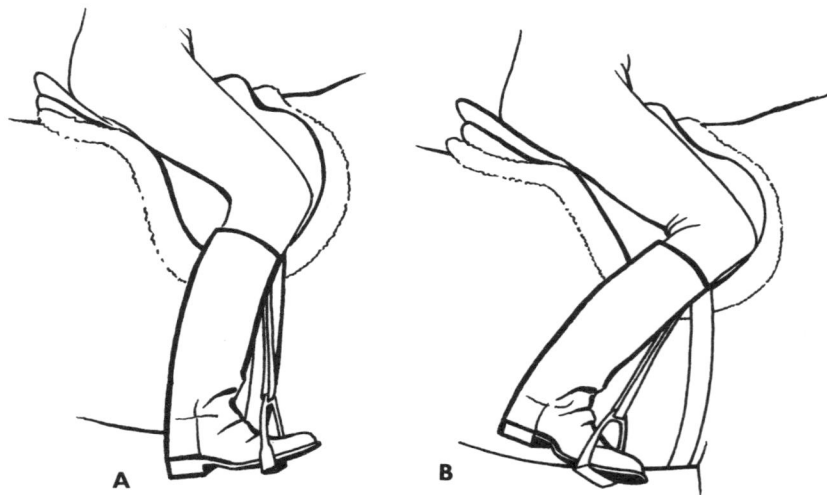

(A) Correct use of leg 'at' the girth, light, inward, tapping action.
(B) Incorrect — leg drawn up and back, toe turned out.

4. Unmounted practice with bit and reins (instructor acting as 'horse'). Good for checking hand position and aids for turns and transitions, following with hands, changing whip.

Effects of poor position or unclear aids must always be pointed out as they occur.

AIDS

Further to the above, teach simple theory of the aids — *Manual No 1*, pages 54–55. Point out that communication and control depend on clear, decisive aids. This is only possible with a steady position, so that hands and legs are not making unintentional movements. They must act as the rider intends, in co-ordination, to apply aids for whatever is required of the pony. The rider's balance and weight distribution can make obedience impossible, or easy, for the pony.

Always check that every member of the ride is sure of the aids for any specific movement or exercise.

Standing trot.

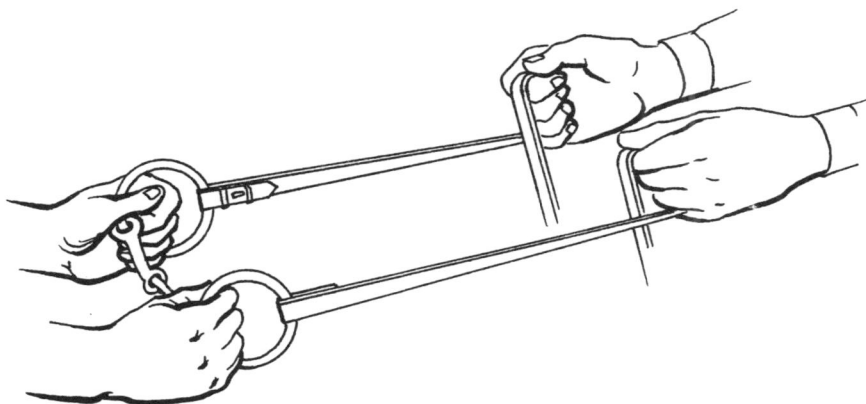

Instructor acting as 'horse'. The bit should always be slightly lower than the 'rider's' hands to give the correct 'feel'.

PONY'S PACES AND WAY OF GOING

Paces are best established on a large circle in the open before going into the school. Trot should be rising, and ponies encouraged to stretch into a light contact.

Work as suggested in *Manual No 1*, pages 62–64. Watch tendency of many ponies to walk too slowly and trot too fast (especially in company). Get riders to count the rhythm out loud.

Divide ride into two sections — one working, one watching. Ask the watchers which ponies show best paces and rhythm. Help the others to improve, then change places. If ponies have fairly even strides, the watchers can clap in rhythm, riders try to keep time. Riding to music (perhaps using a cassette player) is enjoyable and educational.

Never canter the ride all together until you are sure all ponies are under control, but they could probably work in sections of three or four, well spaced out.

At all paces, concentrate first on calmness and regularity, then bend. Teach aids for circles thoroughly here before teaching 20m circles in the school.

Regularity and bend should come before impulsion, except with very sluggish ponies. As balance and suppleness of both pony and rider improve, the rider can begin to use the inside leg (reinforced lightly with whip, if necessary) in rhythm, to encourage the pony to bring the inside hind leg further under and go with more spring and activity — not to be confused with speed.

Ponies should be accepting the bit, as defined in *Manual No 2*, page 27. Some will be coming on the bit as the rider reaches C level, but the instructor must be constantly on guard against attempts to force the pony to come on the bit at the expense of forward movement. Don't even mention collection!

Much of this work will be in trot, but emphasise the importance of walk on a long rein for rest, reward and relaxation. Use trot on long rein to test if the pace is really becoming established.

Changing rein on the large circle may be done either 'through' or 'into' the circle. *Manual No 2*, pages 35–36.

The former is useful as a suppling and change-of-bend exercise, if done correctly, as explained. 'Into' the circle is quicker, and makes riders look and think where they are going. Use both methods for variation.

SUITABLE EXERCISES IN THE SCHOOL AND
WHEN TO INTRODUCE THEM

Corners. Work on these sometimes, as an exercise in sections, with ponies well spaced out. The aim is to maintain the same rhythm round the corners as on the long side. Insist on correct bend, but the corners may be taken quite wide at first, only going deeper as the pony becomes more supple.

Stand at the end of one long side, outside the school. From there, you can check whether the rider is sitting straight, and can see the position of the outside leg. You can also notice whether the pony is straight on the long side.

Mounting and dismounting from either side, altering stirrups and girths, handling a whip, should be taught early in Stage Pre-C1, and must always be done correctly.

SPECIMEN LESSONS

Canter on correct leg on circle. Stage Pre-C1
Reference: *Manual No 1*, pages 61–62.
Prerequisites. Ability to ride at canter. See lesson on page 94. Knowledge of circle aids, and some ability to bend the pony on a large circle.

1. Explain — when the pony canters, his legs on one side appear to be going in front of his legs on the other side. Leader demonstrates canter on a circle during the explanation. Point out that the legs on the inside should always 'lead'. Repeat several times on both reins, and ask members of the ride to say if the pony is cantering correctly.

If possible, show canter on outside leg to emphasise the difference, and how much more awkward it looks and feels. The pony could hit himself, trip or even cross his legs and come down.

2. Explain and demonstrate aids to canter on the inside leg. Emphasise placing of pony, trot a few steps, sitting, look up, sit straight, use both legs, outside leg further back. Ask if everybody understands.

3. Practice. Canter front to rear on large circle, beginning on left rein (easier for many ponies). Tell each rider instantly whether or not the pony is on the correct leg. If 'Yes', praise the pony, if 'No', bring back to trot or walk, check placing and aids, ask again. Praise and pat pony when correct. Encourage rider to feel pony's action, without looking down. Any who fail to get the correct lead after two attempts, rejoin the ride until all have completed the exercise.

4. Demonstrate faults, if necessary. For problems of incorrect canter leads, with the ride lined up, bring the pony out in front of the line to work on a circle approximately 20m. Rider should put whip in outside hand, check own position and placing of pony carefully, ask for canter at the far side of the circle from the ride, using the whip behind the outside leg if unsuccessful first time. When correct, keep going, praising the pony continuously.

In extreme cases, try sending the rider straight out to a marker about 50m from the ride. On reaching it, turn rather sharply back towards the ride, asking for canter at the start of the turn, with the whip in the outside hand. If correct, keep going and praise as above.

When all are successful, repeat on other rein, but this time ask each rider to tell the person in front whether they are correct, as soon as possible after the strike-off.

5. Ask questions — which leg should the pony lead on? Why? Aids?

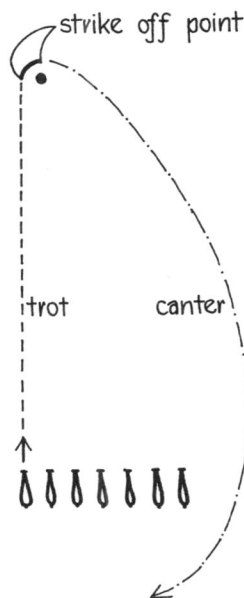

strike off point

trot   canter

The exact place to ask for a strike-off
with a difficult pony.

Practice at home. About six strike-offs every time they ride, with somebody there to tell them if the pony is correct.

Next lesson could be in the school, asking for the strike-off in a corner, and each rider telling the instructor whether the pony strikes off correctly.

A useful exercise. With the ride lined up in the open, place two markers, about 100m apart, 20m in front of the ride. Each person comes out in turn, trots round one of the markers aiming towards the second one. When the pony is on a straight line, the rider shuts his eyes and asks the pony to canter. It won't matter which leg the pony leads on, but the rider should feel his knee on the side of the leading leg moving forward with the pony's shoulder at each stride, and therefore be able to tell the instructor which leg is leading. Point out how important it is to be able to feel this as the pony strikes off, otherwise you cannot praise or correct him quickly enough in training.

20m circles in the school
Reference: *Manual No 1*, pages 75 and 104.
Prerequisites. Knowledge of circle aids. Ability to bend pony on large circles in the open.
Beforehand. Check school — correct size, straight sides, square

corners. Mark X, and true quarter markers, 10m (33ft) from corners on long sides.

1. Form ride up round end of school, explain and demonstrate circle at other end. Emphasise shape — pony touches track at A (or C), at the true quarter markers and goes through X. He does not go into the corners when on the circle. Aids as already taught on large circle in the open. Ask for questions.

2. Walk round school as a ride behind demonstrator and circle at the end. If the ride is very large it may be necessary to work in two sections — you can't fit more than about ten on a 20m circle. Everybody should try it as soon as possible, while it is fresh in their minds. Emphasise again that the circle begins at A or C, you go into the corners before and afterwards but not during the circle.

3. Re-demonstrate shape as necessary, with a little more emphasis on aids and the bend of the ponies. Repeat, and if satisfactory, change the rein.

4. Ask questions, particularly relating to the shape of the circle and the four 'landmarks' that help you to keep it round.

After this rather slow and theoretical lesson for this standard, be sure to do something active — jumping, games or hill work.

Follow-up lessons. Revise above, checking shape and bend, repeat in trot.

Trot front to rear, with a circle at the free end. See page 51. This exercise may also be used to revise regularity of paces throughout, diagonals, aids for circles, corners and transitions.

Remind less experienced riders to sit for the first few strides, check diagonal, where to circle, which corners to go into, look for landmarks, check aids and regularity as necessary, steady in time, sit last few strides. 'Talk' them through it, so that maximum success will be achieved.

Experienced members of the ride work it out for themselves, commenting aloud on good and bad points en route.

Alternatively, explain what you are looking for on each of the above, then ask the ride to watch one another carefully and say who they thought performed the whole exercise well. Useful for revision before C Certificate.

At Stage Pre-C2, circle from B or E. Mark 'crossing points' on centre line, 10m either side of X.

ROAD SAFETY TRAINING

See endpaper for instructional cartoon which shows many of the problems of riding on the road, and could be photocopied and enlarged as a teaching aid. (Permission must be obtained from the publisher before other content of the manuals may be photocopied.)

For practice, mark out a simulated road route in the paddock, including, if possible, road signs and markings, mock traffic lights, pedestrian crossings, etc. Introduce hazards such as parked or moving vehicles or objects on the side of the road which might cause ponies to shy, and teach how to deal with them. *Manual No 1*, page 68.

Make sure that everyone is familiar with 'Riding on the Road', *Manual No 1*, pages 65–68, and has had training before taking part in organised road rides or treks, and also for their own daily safety.

This subject is of the utmost importance — it *must* be taught thoroughly. Any Pony Club official seeing a member showing dangerous or inconsiderate behaviour when 'out and about' should not hesitate to speak to the person in question.

RIDING UP AND DOWN HILL

The ideal place to start is a gently sloping bank, with flat ground top and bottom. The ride works on a large oval, first at walk, then trot, trying to maintain an even pace throughout. Not easy to do, but gives a definite objective — especially important for anyone inclined to be nervous, and vital for control across country.

When trot is established, canter round circuit individually, from front to rear. Don't attempt to canter all together on slopes with rides below C+ level.

As the ride improves and gains confidence, make use of any available slopes, humps and hollows, according to their ability. On steeper gradients, use jumping length stirrups.

Where the Pony Club grounds, and possibly the whole district, are completely flat, try to arrange an occasional outing to another branch or club, a farm or other property where there are hills. Children and ponies who work only on the flat can be terrified of the slightest slope, and the improvement in both from working on undulating ground can be immediate and remarkable. It is obviously essential to be able to ride, before attempting to jump, up and down hill.

Remember, this is hard work for ponies who are not very fit, or are unaccustomed to hills, so don't overdo it. Allow plenty of rests at walk on a long rein on the flat in between times, and for cooling down at the end.

TAKING RIDES 'OUT'

While it is realised that this may appear an 'impossible dream' for some urban clubs, whose grounds are virtually surrounded by motorways and other major highways, there is no doubt that well-organised rides can be invaluable at this stage.

Taking rides out is the best way of:

1. Teaching everything in 'Out and About with your Pony', *Manual No 1*, Chapter 5, in a completely practical way. Safety on the road, courtesy to other road users, riders and pedestrians, and the well-being of the pony.

2. Giving a change from the more formal tuition at most rallies, providing fun and education in equal measure.

3. Preparing for treks, hunting, horse trials and other strenuous activities, teaching children how to exercise their ponies from the point of view of getting them fit. Developing a feel for speed and distance.

4. Discovering the joys of riding and seeing the countryside from the back of a pony — endangered in these days of intense competition.

Organising rides

1. Be sure that all members can control their ponies round the Pony Club grounds before taking them further afield. They should have been introduced to the foregoing activities.

2. Always plan and time the route beforehand. It will probably take longer than you think, especially with a big ride. Aim to include some distance on a quiet road, and some farmland, forestry, beach or whatever is available. Obtain permission, where necessary. Let somebody in authority know where you are going.

3. You will need one mounted assistant (junior instructor or older member), to every four or five children. It can be useful to have a leading rein in your pocket.

4. On the road, arrange the ride two abreast in groups of four, with a gap in between to allow vehicles to fit in. Young or nervous ponies on the inside, with a quiet one between them and the traffic. Have an assistant in front to set the pace, and ride at the back yourself, where you can see what is happening.

5. Keep order in open paddocks or on the beach. Don't allow any cantering until all are settled in trot. The first canter is best away from home, slightly uphill if possible — impetuous ponies to go first,

one at a time. Make use (with permission) of any logs, small ditches or other obstacles for those who wish, and are capable, to have a 'go'.
6. Take every opportunity to point out anything of interest — stock, birds, trees, crops, good and bad plants to have in your paddock, noxious or poisonous plants, fences, gates. Ask, 'Would this be a good paddock to keep your pony in?' Divide into two teams, one to spot good points, one bad.
7. In the latter stages, be sure that riders keep together, and walk, so that ponies arrive back cool.

OPENING AND SHUTTING GATES

Reference: *Manual No 1*, pages 68–69.
Apart from technique, points to emphasise include:
1. If anyone dismounts to open a gate, out hunting, for instance, at least one other person must stay with them until they have remounted, otherwise their horse won't stand.
2. How a mounted rider should hold a gate for others to pass through. Practise passing through in succession, not letting the gate swing on the next person.

JUMPING, PRE-C

Reference: *Manual No 1*, Chapter 6, and pages 65–74 of this book. If the instructor is unmounted, a competent, well-mounted assistant who can demonstrate, particularly in the initial stages, is invaluable. Revise or introduce the work over poles on the ground, page 95.

JUMPING POSITION

Reference: *Manual No 1*, pages 84–85.
Overall picture: stirrups one or two holes shorter than on the flat, the angles at hip, knee and ankle will be a little more acute. Contact maintained with hand and lower leg. Pony's paces and rhythm as on the flat.
Check:
1. Head up, looking where going.
2. Body slightly forward — vertical line, shoulder, knee and toe.
3. Seat pushed back a little, (because knee is higher) in light contact with saddle, but weight forward over knees, stirrups and heels. Inside of the calf in contact with pony's side, heels well down.
4. Reins will be shorter, because the body is further forward. Hands either side of, and close to, the pony's neck. Straight line from elbow to bit must be retained, with reins and whip correctly held.

FIRST JUMPING LESSONS

Place each rider individually in the jumping position at halt. Emphasise the importance of stretching down with weight into the heel to maintain balance. Ask each to put reins in one hand, the other hand flat on the pony's neck, over the neckstrap but not holding it unless required. This will be the position over the jump. Briefly explain reasons for forward position.

Practise jumping position on the flat on the large circle in walk and steady, rising trot. Also maintaining the position on transitions and over 'scattered' trotting poles, *Manual No 1*, page 80, with reins in both hands.

For the first lesson put two poles together between stands by a fence line, and let the ride walk and trot over them in single file, about six lengths apart. In the last few strides they should put the reins in one hand, the other hand on the neck or neckstrap — as though they were jumping. Check that the rider remains straight and does not drop the shoulder.

It is best to do this work going away from home, especially if there are excitable ponies in the ride. These ponies should be tucked in close behind a steady leader, not at the back of the ride. In extreme cases they may have to be taken individually, or even led, and they will certainly have to be kept to ground poles for quite a long time. Such ponies are unsuitable for beginners learning to jump, and quickly cause loss of confidence. The problem should be discussed with the Head Instructor and parents.

Next, make the poles into a small cross with ground-line, no more than 30cm (1ft) in the centre. About 3m (10ft) before the jump, the rider puts the reins into one hand, the other hand on the neck (or neckstrap). The hand holding the reins should go slightly forward, so that, for the moment, there is no contact and the pony is completely free to use his head and neck. On landing, the reins are taken up again in both hands and the pony ridden straight forward. Demonstrate.

To finish with, line the ride up facing the jump and have riders jump one at a time. It can be helpful to have three markers, one 15–20m either side of the jump, to ensure a straight approach and departure, and one at the point where the reins are to be put in one hand. Demonstrate.

If the preliminary work has been thoroughly taught, few children should have any trouble provided they have a suitable pony.

Practice at home. Practise jumping position on the flat in walk and trot, and a small jump, no bigger than in class. Only five or six jumps a day, three days a week. Remind riders to let stirrups down after jumping. Suggest all read *Manual No 1*, pages 78–79.

Next lesson. Revise jumping position at walk and trot, and in a canter from front to rear on a large circle. Emphasise lower leg must be steady, weight going down through knee and stirrup into heel.

Introduce three trotting poles, *Manual No 1*, page 82.

Repeat previous jump, first with hand on neck, then, as riders become steady and confident, with reins in both hands. Be sure the hands follow freely forward so that there is no interference with the pony's mouth. Don't worry if contact is lost at this stage. If anybody gets 'left behind', explain what happened and repeat the jump immediately, holding the neckstrap.

Change fence to a horizontal pole about 40cm (16in), with ground-line, and jump individually. This will go more smoothly if ponies canter the last few strides, back to trot afterwards. Think of straight-ness, rider's position and freedom of pony's head and neck over the fence, control. The ride watching and commenting on these factors. Finish with a good effort by each rider.

Practice at home. Jumping position at walk, trot and canter. Three trotting poles, check that each knows distance for own pony. Single jump, cross or horizontal, as above. Read *Manual No 1*, pages 82–85.

Lesson. Revise trotting poles, fill gaps. Concentrate on rhythm and bend when circling either way. Put single, small fence beside poles, use alternately, keeping same pace and contact over both.

Lesson. Three in a line Reference: *Manual No 1*, pages 85–86.

'Walk the course' with riders mounted, deciding the exact 'track', where to start each turn to ensure a smooth curve and a straight approach. Explain the use of 'landmarks' to help with this. Drawing the track on a blackboard set up in the jumping area can also be useful. Demonstrate riding a correct track.

Each rider then jumps the three fences, very small, individually at trot. If the track is incorrect, he continues until it is right. Those who did a good first round may have fences a little bigger and canter the last few strides, but should still trot round turns, to ensure control and accuracy. Check that the forward position is maintained throughout, and that there is contact with hand and leg between fences, using the lower leg lightly in rhythm in front of the fence.

Practice at home. According to performance. All practise jumping position, trotting over four or five poles, closed up. Those not yet proficient at riding a correct track should practise over poles on the ground in 'three in a line' layout. Others may practise three in a line, if jumps are available, twice a week. Jumps no bigger than in class. All read *Manual No 1*, pages 86–87. Study pictures of the phases of the jump.

Lesson. About four fences arranged as an easy, flowing course. One fence could have a row of small drums or hay bales, one crossed poles with a horizontal on the landing side, making a slight spread. Walk the course, as in the previous lesson, emphasising how smoothly it will ride if you follow the correct track. Practise each fence separately, checking approach and position. When riding the course, canter the last few strides, but still trot round turns. With fences at about 45cm (18in) all should achieve smooth clear rounds, if the teaching to date has been sound.

Practice at home. Practise jumping position, trotting poles with single fence beside them, small course of similar type if fences available. Stress that control is the first essential. Then work towards maintaining a steady, regular canter.

From now on, courses may be increased gradually in length and may include all types of fences, spread and upright, and combinations, up to C Certificate height of 60cm (2ft), or occasionally bigger for those who are capable.

STARTING CROSS-COUNTRY

Prerequisites:
1. Ability of rider and pony to jump small, varied show-jumping courses up to 60cm (2ft) at canter.
2. Ability to ride up and down hill, with control, at walk, trot and canter.
3. Availability of suitable fences up to 60cm (2ft) within a fairly small area. They must all be within sight and sound of the instructor (with loud-hailer, if necessary). A cross-country *course* is useless for starting. See page 202 for suggestions.

An experienced older member on a free-going horse or pony can be invaluable, both as demonstrator and for giving leads when required.

Always check girths especially carefully at the start of a cross-country lesson.

During the work-in, make sure that everybody can control their pony when cantering in the open, both on the flat and on undulating ground. Show how to steady an excitable pony. See *Manual No 2*, page 53.

Then practise over a simple and inviting fence, such as a log or a brush, on the flat, making a long approach and maintaining a regular canter in front of the fence and on the 'getaway', pulling up smoothly and returning to the ride at walk. Repeat until every pony does it calmly and evenly, without haste or hesitation.

Next work over one or more different types of fences, as follows.

Fences on slopes

Emphasise: Uphill, rider *must* keep well forward throughout and give the pony plenty of rein. Hold mane or neckstrap if there is any tendency to be 'left behind'.

Downhill. Approach at trot until certain of control. Head up, heels down, body not too far forward — all especially important to maintain balance.

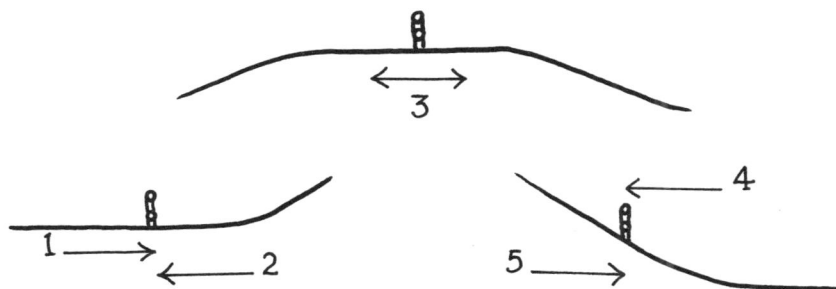

Introducing small fences on slopes. (1) Easy. (2) Needs more control than 1. (3) Rider must have steady position. (4) Needs impulsion, not speed, rider must have good balance. (5) Needs control, firm position, courage.

Banks

An ideal type of bank for Pony Club use is shown on page 204.

Start by riding across the low end, approaching in trot, with the ride about six lengths apart. Any pony stopping must step up from a standstill. Those behind circle away and continue when the way is clear. Failing this, make use of any suitable small ledges for jumping up and down.

Technique as for jumping on slopes — going up, well forward, plenty of rein, jumping down, more upright.

Ditches

Start with a small ditch, see page 205.

Practise in groups of three or four, about six lengths apart, with an experienced pony as leader of each group. They should go towards home and the other ponies.

Emphasise looking up over the ditch, not down into it, keep well forward, hold mane or neckstrap if necessary. Steady approach until the last few strides, then, when the pony has seen the ditch, push him on firmly. Use voice for *quiet* encouragement.

If a pony stops, he must not be allowed to turn away, but must go over from a standstill. Another pony could come past to give a lead, or the instructor could hop over first, not getting directly in front of the pony. Praise at once when he goes, then repeat until he jumps confidently, dismount and reward with a titbit.

When all are used to the plain ditch, put a low pole over the centre first, then on the take-off, and finally on the landing, side. Miniature 'coffin' type obstacles should also be introduced.

Free-going fences

Logs of various sizes are invaluable, as are small, well-built spreads. Jump at a steady, active canter.

Obstacles in fence lines

Start with a very small spar or post and rails. See page 203. These fences can cause problems with ponies unaccustomed to them, but are essential for hunting or eventing. First be sure that all riders and ponies are jumping confidently over obstacles slightly bigger than the present fence. Jump towards home, in groups as above.

When all are familiar with the different types of fences individually, make up a short course, aiming to keep a controlled canter throughout.

As riders progress, a good exercise is to time the first round, then, if the pace is satisfactory, let them see how close they can get to the same time on the second round. This begins to give a feel for pace without racing.

FOUNDATIONS

These early stages of jumping are extremely important. Bad habits allowed to become established at the beginning will prove very difficult indeed to overcome later on.

Many young riders (and some parents) believe that 'big is beautiful', and the instructor will have to think up a variety of exercises and problems, involving siting of fences and use of terrain, to make the essential fundamentals enjoyable and challenging.

Riders who are ready to tackle bigger fences should certainly be allowed to do so, but not continually, and only when the instructor is certain that the partnership is capable.

If the training is progressive, always consolidating before going on to a more advanced stage or bigger fences, there should not be problems of ponies stopping or running out, or riders falling off. If these things happen frequently, the instructor must look hard at his training methods. Also talk to riders and parents and try to find out what individual jumping practice is being done at home. Too much or too big can undo everything taught at Pony Club.

Those who arrive at Pony Club having already done a considerable amount of jumping but are not up to C standard, and on incorrect lines, need tactful handling. It is essential to convince them of the necessity for sound foundations if they wish to be really successful with their jumping, or to gain their Pony Club certificates.

GAMES

Games, both for instructional purposes and purely for fun, should still form a major part of the activities for Post-D riders.

Many of the games suggested in Chapter 3 will still be popular, and these can be played at a higher level — e.g., canter, rather than trot.

A useful variation on the 'musical chairs' theme is 'musical mounting'. When the music stops (or whistle sounds) riders dismount on the right, run round the front of the pony, and mount on the left. Last one up is 'out'. At the next halt, change sides — dismount on left, mount on right. Vaulting on is permitted, and may be specified if the ride is learning to vault.

Scavenger hunts may become more 'technical', with riders searching for good or bad grasses, poisonous plants or other things they would or would not like to have in their paddocks. A few specimens to show at the start would be valuable.

The gymkhana practice suggested in *Manual No 1*, pages 96–97, should provide further ideas for instructors, as should the NZPCA booklet, *The Pony Club Mounted Games*, and the British Horse Society's *Mounted Games and Gymkhanas*.

Polocrosse may be started at about C level, with equipment, and a competent person to teach the basic skills of picking up, carrying, throwing and catching the ball. Lack of such tuition in the initial stages will result in great frustration, but once some degree of skill is acquired many simple games and exercises can be devised for practice and enjoyment, before attempting a full-scale match.

As always, a quiet start in a calm atmosphere will ensure understanding, and will go a long way to avoid unnecessary roughness later on in the heat of competition.

The Polocrosse Council of New Zealand puts out an excellent rulebook, and its members are always willing to assist Pony Clubs who wish to play the game.

Paper chases, treasure hunts or mock hunts are all enjoyable and educational, provided riders and ponies are fit and competent, and sufficient help is available.

CARE OF THE PONY

Lessons at this standard should relate to the riders' own ponies. It is essential that members should be shown how to do even the simplest things correctly, and that they should practise them under supervision.

SPECIMEN LESSONS

Grooming — Stage Pre-C1
Reference: *Manual No 1*, pages 145–148.
Requirements: A quiet pony, suitable size. Grooming kit, bucket of water.
1. Introduce: 'Today we are going to show how to groom a pony. The pony should always be tied up correctly. First remove your hat and coat.' Show and name the grooming tools.
2. Demonstrate and explain: Correct approach, how to hold and use the tools, reasons for grooming. Invite questions.
3. Practice: Members of the ride come out in pairs to practise different aspects of the lesson. Re-demonstrate or assist as necessary.
4. Prove lesson by asking questions.
Follow-up. A special check on grooming at the next rally.

Recognition and Uses of Feedstuffs — Stage Pre-C3
Reference: *Manual No 1*, pages 128–131.
Requirements: Samples of hay — meadow and lucerne. Hard feed — pony pellets, chaff, bran, oats, bruised and whole, barley. 'Extras' — molasses, salt, carrots, correctly sliced.
1. Explain: Why ponies need bulk and/or hard feed. The importance of choosing the best feed for individual ponies.
2. Show: How to recognise feedstuffs, and explain their uses. Do not be too technical, be sure to relate to the age-group. Suggest suitable

types of feed for each member's pony. Invite questions throughout.
3. Prove the lesson by asking questions, particularly in relation to recognition of feeds, and their suitability for different ponies.
Follow-up. Ask each member to write down what feed their pony is getting, and to bring their feed table to the next rally.

USE OF THE SYLLABUS

The syllabus for C Certificate is outlined on pages 22–25. The following suggestions are made to help instructors to plan the order in which they will teach the lessons and general work, and to devise six-rally plans for each of the phases.

STAGE PRE-C1

Riding
Inspection — more work to be done by the rider.
Position. Reasons for maintaining the correct position.
Rising, sitting trot. Short trots without stirrups, holding pommel.
Exercises, halt and walk, position and activity.
Aids. Better understanding and co-ordination in applying the aids
    for transitions, turns and circles.
Revise and confirm: Reins in one hand. Walk on long rein. Canter,
    position and control.
Lessons: Mount and dismount on right side.
Altering stirrups, tightening girth, mounted.
Circle aids on large circle in the open.
Diagonals.
Canter on correct leg on circle.
The pony's paces and rhythm.
Riding up and down gentle slopes at walk and trot.
Riding on the road, correct side, hand signals.
Games.

Jumping
Revise walk/trot over scattered poles.
Lessons: Jumping position on flat and over single small fence.
Poles on the ground.
Three in a line, or other very simple course of three or four fences,
    canter last few strides only.

5-minute talks
Handling a whip — best type to use.
Aids, natural and artificial.

Own ponies' bits.
Does your pony need shoeing?
Further points of the pony.
Terms and expressions used in the school.

Care of the pony and other instruction
Lessons: Requirements of a pony at grass.
Care with the change of seasons.
Feeding hay.
Reasons for grooming, use and care of tools.
Picking up and picking out the feet (forefeet only if owner is small
    and pony large or restless).
Putting on and taking off a cover.
Signs of good and bad health — recognise obvious lameness or ill-
    health.
When to ask advice.
Saddling up and fitting of own pony's tack.
Tack cleaning.
Leading in hand at trot and turning.
Own Pony Club, its branches and other clubs nearby.

STAGE PRE-C2

Riding
Inspection. Higher standard of grooming/tack cleaning.
Position. Further exercises. Short trots minus stirrups, without
    holding saddle, if capable.
Revise and confirm Stage Pre-C1.
Improve application and accuracy of aids. Use of whip to reinforce
    leg on transitions and circles.
Further work on undulating ground, including canter.
Lessons: Free forward movement, accepting the bit.
Trot on long rein.
20m circles.
Halt, salute.
Opening and shutting gates, dismounted/mounted.
Riding on the road — road signs, passing stationary vehicles, pony
    shying on road.
Games.

Jumping
Improve position and contact over poles and fences.
Lessons: Jumping at trot and canter.

Jumping without reins.

Two-stride doubles.

Walking a course and riding it with improved rhythm, bend and more accurate track.

Jumps at top and bottom of gentle slope.

Jumping on and off a low bank.

5-minute talks

The pony's balance.

Training and the mind of the pony (very simply).

Junior riding tests.

The pony's foot.

Care of the pony and other instruction

Lessons: Choosing a paddock and daily care thereof.

Elementary watering and feeding, including pellets and chaff.

Better grooming — use of body brush, picking out feet.

Types of shoes.

Dosing for worms — why, when, what to give.

Rasping teeth — which teeth need rasping and why.

Coughs, colds, isolation.

Colic.

Minor wounds, first-aid kit.

Knowledge of Pony Club.

Behaviour when out and about.

STAGE PRE-C3

Riding

Inspection — turnout of a consistently good standard.

Position — continue to improve. Stress necessity for good position in order to apply aids accurately, so that the pony will understand and obey. Point out effects of poor position on pony's work.

A few exercises at trot. Short canter without stirrups.

Revise and confirm previous stage. Develop feel for diagonals, leading leg, etc.

Lessons: Footfalls at all paces.

20m circles at canter.

Junior riding test.

Strong canter in the open, pull up.

Riding through water.

Games.

Jumping
Lessons: Jump after trotting poles.
One-stride doubles, small bounce.
Small fences on slopes, ditches.
Walk and ride introductory grade cross-country and show-jumping
    courses.

Care of the pony and other instruction
Rules of good feeding, recognition of feedstuffs.
Feeding and exercise — own pony's programme.
Condition and fitness for work required.
Loading and unloading — how to lead the pony on and off the
    float.
Laminitis and grass staggers.
Lice, ticks, ringworm.
Kicks, bruises, injuries from tack — bit, saddle, cover, etc.
Care of pony at a show or event.

5
TEACHING INTERMEDIATE RIDERS
C to B CERTIFICATES

A well-turned-out B level jumping ride.

B standard represents a big step forward in a member's career — the transition from the comparatively passive rider to the active, thinking horseman or woman, who can improve a horse's performance and way of going, ride any reasonably well-mannered horse or pony, and, if desired, compete at more advanced levels.

The rider must be able to turn the horse out well, in suitable condition for whatever activities are required, and to care for it competently at home or when travelling. For this, a deeper knowledge of all aspects of horse management is necessary.

Members should be learning more about Pony Club, its objects, organisation and standards, and developing a responsible and considerate attitude.

The interim test, C+, is in itself a worthwhile goal. It marks the time when riders begin to assess and think for themselves, but it does not demand great technical skill or jumping ability. It is within reach of any rider with an average horse or pony, and the will to succeed.

CRITERIA FOR INSTRUCTORS

Experience of teaching at lower levels.

B course with a National Instructor, or possibly an Association course.

Attendance at a C+ or B examiners' clinic as an observer, writing for dressage judges and assisting a good designer in building jumping courses can all be most helpful.

Study and observation of riders at these levels. Attendance at competitions, examinations, courses. (Assess and analyse the reasons for success or failure and try to relate what you see to the principles in *Manuals 1* and *2*.)

A clear, analytical mind to help riders to recognise their own and their horses' good and bad points, and to decide objectively, if problems occur, where the weakness lies.

It is desirable that instructors at this level should be riders themselves, able at least to attempt the work on the flat, or that they should have ridden to this standard in the past, so that they will appreciate the problems involved. Nevertheless, there are some who do not ride, but have learnt a great deal through their children's riding activities, and can give much help to C+ and B riders.

Practical experience of horse management, particularly in the areas of getting horses fit, travelling and stabling.

Any specialised knowledge of eventing, showing or other branches of riding is valuable at this stage.

INSTRUCTOR'S OBJECTIVES

1. Understanding. To broaden the rider's knowledge of:

(a) The paces, the terms relating to the horse's way of going and the theory and use of the aids.

(b) Assessing progress, and the work needed by rider and horse for further improvement.

(c) The relationship between dressage and jumping.

(d) How to build good fences which will develop the horse's confidence and style.

(e) The horse's conformation, health and well-being, and what is needed to condition and prepare him for a variety of activities.

(f) Pony Club, its objects and standards.

2. Technique:

(a) To improve the security, balance and steadiness of the rider's position, enabling him to begin to make use of seat and weight aids, and to apply all the aids with greater finesse.

(b) To develop the jumping position, so that it becomes stronger and more adaptable to differing circumstances and types of fences.

(c) To teach how to ride at the gallop, and to acquire practical knowledge of pace and distance.

3. Control. For the rider to be in full control of his own mount, and to be able to manage any unknown but reasonably well-mannered horse.

Problems

Both instructor and pupils, especially when first starting on this work, being overawed by the prospect of what lies ahead. C+ is invaluable in this connection. Riders must be helped to develop habits of thought and self-analysis if they are to enjoy more advanced work.

Members at this stage can become narrow-minded and totally competition-orientated. Every effort must be made to stimulate interest in all branches of riding, rather than encouraging too much specialisation. The instructor's, and parents', attitudes, the variety and the challenges offered are all-important in maintaining the interest of this age-group.

STAGES PRE-B1 AND 2 (UP TO C+)

The start of a more technical approach to riding. Be sure to 'keep it simple' and not make a sudden change in the teaching. Try to involve pupils and get them asking for information, rather than thrusting it upon them. Demonstrate yourself, or use older members to demonstrate the horse's way of going (accepting/on the bit, etc.) and new movements.

A short session of watching a good video, followed immediately by practical application, can be helpful.

Encourage gradual lengthening of stirrups, and more work without them.

Constantly check the straightness of horse and rider, and all the points detailed in the previous chapter (page 106).

Make use of movements such as circles, serpentines, etc, transitions, lengthening and shortening of stride, to improve both the rider's co-ordination and the pony's way of going.

Encourage comment and discussion, both on their own and other people's work.

Ask riders to suggest useful exercises for themselves and their ponies, and help them to plan their training programmes. *Manual No 2*, pages 33–34.

Individual work is valuable when the number in the ride permits, but can become too intensive if overdone at this stage.

SUITABLE EXERCISES IN THE SCHOOL

In addition to those listed for C, in which a higher standard of performance can be expected.

TEACHING NEW MOVEMENTS

For C+, these comprise 15m and 10m circles, serpentines, a few lengthened strides in trot, turn on the forehand and change of leg through the trot.

Notice how these movements are set out in *Manual No 2*:
1. A definition of the movement.
2. The objects of the exercise.
3. When to introduce it.
4. The pace or paces at which it may be performed.
5. Method and aids.
6. How it should feel.
7. Common faults and corrections.

From the teaching point of view, the first consideration is No 3, whether riders and horses are ready to start the movement. Excitable and undisciplined horses can easily become confused if new movements are introduced before the basics are established.

Nos 1, 2 and 5 will form the basis of the initial explanation and demonstration. It is essential that everybody understands the objects of the exercise and the benefits to be gained from it, so that these movements will be practised sensibly.

No 4. When starting a new movement both rider and horse need time to work out what is required, without tension. Therefore, whatever pace will ultimately be most beneficial, always begin at walk.

No 6, 'feel', is of the utmost importance. The instructor must be able to recognise, and tell the rider, *as he is working,* when he is on the right lines, and the exact moment when he finally achieves the desired result. Once a rider has experienced the 'feel' of the movement correctly executed he will know what to aim for, and be able to continue profitably with practice at home.

No 7, common faults. Note how often these stem from poor balance and/or poor co-ordination of aids.

SPECIMEN LESSONS

Lengthening the stride in trot — Stage Pre-B1
Reference: *Manual No 2,* pages 40–42.

An introductory lesson, particularly suited to the 12–14 age-group, and to ponies, who often have greater difficulty in lengthening the stride than do horses. Could easily be commenced in Stage Pre-C3.

Notice that this lesson is unusual in that there is no demonstration and very little explanation, the emphasis being on practice and 'feel'.

Work on a very large circle, widely spaced, in the open. First establish the working trot, then tell the ride to slow it down until the ponies are *just* trotting. This means that riders will have to use legs to maintain the pace and hands to steady it. Build up to working trot again. Do this several times, and then, from the working trot, tell the ride to 'trot on'. Speed does not matter at this early stage. Riders should close the legs steadily and allow their ponies to take the necessary rein. After a few strides back to working trot. Alternate slow, working and 'lengthened' pace. Ponies usually respond well, and the riders get the feel of what is required without becoming too technical.

Now explain the objects of these adjustments of stride, and how it relates to stride control in jumping. (Appeals to this age-group!)

A more formal lesson in the school. Prerequisite: a calm and reasonably well-established working trot.
1. Explain the objects of the exercise.
2. Demonstrate a few (four or five) lengthened strides on one long side, with the ride lined up opposite. Draw attention to the preparation, and the clear transitions within the pace. Point out that seat and leg always precede hand on these transitions, and how the hands

follow forward to 'allow' the lengthening. Explain that ponies in particular may initially *have* to increase the speed a little — the first essential is to produce some difference in the stride. Ask for questions.

3. Practice. Must be in open order — in two sections, if necessary, so that you can watch riders individually and tell them immediately they attain even two or three satisfactory strides. Praise pony and bring back to working pace before balance is lost.

4. Re-demonstrate as required.

5. Further practice. This time, ask the riders to tell you when they can feel some lengthening.

6. Prove the lesson. Advise on individual practice at home. Remind all not to ask too much — maximum four or five strides and bring the pony back before he loses his balance and begins to 'run' or breaks.

Several short 'lengthenings' are much better than one long one in these early stages. Practise on the long side of the school or on a fence line to help in keeping the pony straight.

Pre-B3. Another useful exercise may be carried out on an oval on a gentle slope. Riders sit going down, which is easy and comfortable for both parties, since the force of gravity slides the rider down in the saddle and helps to bring the pony's hocks under him. Make a half-circle about 15m at the bottom of the slope, then ask for lengthening uphill, rising as the pony responds. Results can be quite striking in the increased use of hocks and shoulders as the pony stretches out up the slope. Do not ask for lengthening downhill, which would encourage falling on the forehand and put strain on the forelegs.

JUDGMENT OF SPEED AND DISTANCE

Reference: *Manual No 2*, pages 51–52.

This may be taught in the paddock or on rides out, over measured distances on quiet roads, for the slower paces. The latter is specially useful for members who are learning to get their ponies fit for hunting, horse trials or long-distance rides.

Gallop, *Manual No 2*, pages 52–54. Much enjoyed by C+ riders, but it is essential for their own safety and that of others that they should be taught how, when and where to do it!

RIDING UNKNOWN PONIES

Reference: *Manual No 2*, pages 54–55.
May be commenced at this stage, by exchanging suitable ponies on the flat, possibly in the school initially. *Note*: Changing ponies is not required for the C+ examination.

JUMPING

Reference: *Manual No 2*, Chapter 4.
At this stage, the rider's position on the flat and over fences should become more established and distinctive, so there will be a greater difference in stirrup length. This depends to some extent on the saddle and the rider's build, but will usually be at least two or three holes, and possibly more for cross-country.

The instructor's first aims should be to correct and strengthen the jumping position, using the methods outlined in *Manual No 2*, pages 60–61. Riders should be made aware of the 'check points' and the effects of faulty positions — pages 56–60.

Increased attention should be paid to contact over the fence. Point out that the grey horse in the pictures on pages 57 and 59 is the same animal, and what a difference the rider's hands and contact can make to the horse's style and comfort.

Have your ride assist with building fences or a course at a rally, and explain the types of fences and the reasons for placing them where they are. Discuss distances in combinations, teach riders to pace them out, to understand the problems that could arise and how to make essential adjustments for their own ponies.

Riders should be taught to recognise their own pony's faults in jumping, and how to go about correcting them. *Manual No 2*, pages 77-81. Stress the importance of using trotting poles and simple jumping and gymnastic exercises. The variations of the exercise on page 67 and of the 'box' on page 70 are most useful. Another good exercise is jumping a single fence on a circle of approximately 30m diameter. The bend and canter lead must be maintained on both reins.

CROSS-COUNTRY

Reference: *Manual No 2*, pages 73–76, and *Manual No 3*, pages 120–122.

Continue cross-country training with greater variety of fences and terrain, e.g., jumping into water, slightly steeper hills and bigger drops. *Note*: Only on good going and not too many. One successful effort is enough.

Explain the principles of alternative fences, and how to decide what would be best for one's own pony.

Cross-country pace should be becoming more consistent, and riders concentrating on taking the shortest possible track, while allowing sufficient straight strides on the approach to the fence.

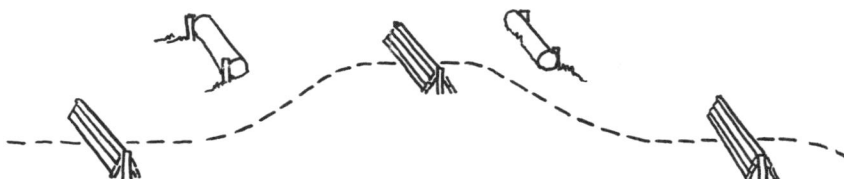

Exercises on slopes, suitable for C+ level. All fences to be jumpable either way. 'Hen-coops' in line, logs offset to one side. Fences should be jumped individually before continuing to the related fence(s) in that line.

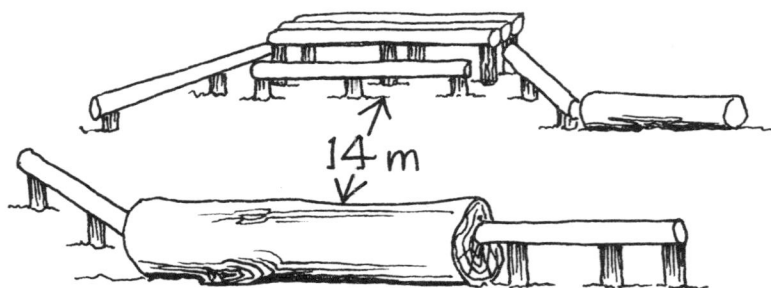

14 m

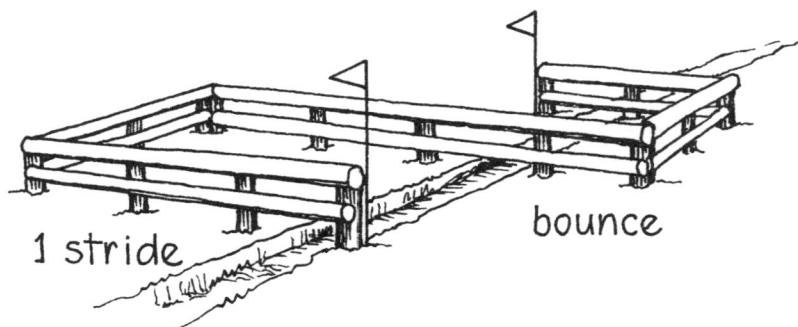

1 stride

bounce

Useful training alternatives.

GAMES

At C+ level quite a marked division may develop in members' attitudes towards games. Some riders may feel that they have out-grown them, and/or that they may be detrimental to their ponies training for eventing or other competitive work. Others still enjoy games immensely, perhaps for their chosen form of competition, or just for fun and relaxation.

There is something to be said for both points of view. It is obviously true that excessive galloping and racing will make 'hot' ponies worse and young ones confused, but relaxation *is* important, and if games are carefully chosen they can offer challenge and enjoyment for the majority. For example, most of the rally relays and mounted games listed in Chapters 5 and 6 of *Mounted Games and Gymkhanas.*

Slow chukkas of polocrosse or cushion polo, steady training for barrel racing — essential for success — will appeal to some members.

Others will enjoy a team jumping competition on the lines of a Nations Cup, with the most junior riders of each team going first, and fences adjusted according to ability.

Musical and activity rides are another possibility at this level.

PONY MANAGEMENT

More specialised knowledge is required of conditioning and all that goes with it — feeding, grooming, exercise, etc. — and of carrying out prescribed veterinary treatments.

Keep the teaching practical — do it, don't just talk about it! Make use of older members to demonstrate or to take individuals or small groups, as, for instance, in horse management workshops. See page 76.

SPECIMEN LESSON

Condition — Stage Pre-B1

Reference: *Manual No 1*, pages 136–137, and *Manual No 2*, pages 88–92.

This subject is much too big to be taught in one lesson. The following is suggested as an introduction.

Requirements: one pony in big condition, one reasonably fit — e.g., competing in pre-training or training level trials. Suitable daily rations for each pony.

Point out where the fat lies on the 'big' pony — on the crest, either side of the spine, on the hindquarters and belly. Explain the probable effects on his lungs and legs if he were to be worked hard in his present state, or to get fatter.

Contrast this with the outline and muscular development of the fitter pony, particularly on the neck, shoulders, hindquarters, forearm and thigh. Encourage pupils to feel the difference as well as observing it.

Then suggest and discuss suitable feeding and exercise programmes for each pony. Give reasons for the type and amount of feed and exercise, and relate this to the class's own ponies and any conditioning problems they may have. Draw attention to the third element in conditioning — thorough daily strapping.

Ask the class to estimate their ponies' present condition, and each to bring a similar feed and exercise programme to the next rally, with some indication of how they will expect to develop the programme if they wish to get their pony fitter. Also to bring grooming kit for a lesson on strapping.

STAGES PRE-B3 AND PRE-B4, UP TO B CERTIFICATE

Rides are fairly sure to be smaller at this level, allowing for more individual work. Pupils should now be ready for this. The approach can be less formal, with riders doing much of the work in their own time, and emphasis on discussion. Encourage riders to 'talk as they work', saying when they think and feel that the horse is going well or performing a movement correctly.

Watch constantly for straightness, calm, free, forward movement, rhythm and a steady head carriage in the horse, with improving balance and impulsion.

During, and as a result of, the work towards B Certificate and the development of the rider's position and feel, the horse should advance from the acceptance of the bit at C+ level, to the stage when he begins to come on the bit in the true meaning of the term. See *Manual No 2*, page 27.

Riders should understand the importance of improving their own ability, and the difficulties that faulty positions and unclear aids can cause. They require considerable motivation to practise the necessary physical exercises and work without stirrups regularly at home.

New movements for B Certificate are riding in position, decrease and increase of circle, canter from walk and the early stages of demi-pirouette.

It is possible at this level that no demonstrator or video will be available. In this case, first study and discuss with the class the text

138

and illustrations for that movement in *Manual No 2*. Make especially sure that everybody is clear about the aids and how the movement should look and feel. You will often find that, following this discussion, at least one person will produce good enough results to enable you to 'talk them through it' in a demonstration.

At the end of the first lesson, if you have any doubts as to whether riders can continue on the right lines at home, it would be best to advise them not to attempt to carry out the movement on their own, but to re-read it before the next rally.

SPECIMEN LESSONS

Decrease and increase of circle — Stage Pre-B3
Reference: *Manual No 2*, pages 37–38.
Prerequisites: the horse must be responsive to the leg in the turn on the forehand, and capable of 10–15m circles in trot.
1. Explain. This exercise follows on from the turn on the forehand, confirming the rider's ability to use the legs independently, and the horse's response to this use of leg, thereby preparing both for lateral work.
2. Demonstrate the movement at one end of the school, starting on a 20m circle, reducing to about 15m, at walk. Ask for questions.
3. Practise in sections of two or three, the others watching and commenting. Look for the straightness of the rider and light, clear leg aids, and be sure the horse is stepping away from the leg to increase the circle.

Common faults are:

(a) Quarters swinging out, mainly caused by using the inside leg too far back.

(b) Falling in, or failing to move away on the increase of circle, usually caused by 'clamping' with the inside leg. This often leads to the rider dropping the inside shoulder and sitting to the outside. Emphasise use of whip to reinforce leg if necessary. Dressage whips can be helpful at this stage.

Failure to move out may also be due to unclear rein aids. A half-halt, coupled with a slight indication of the required direction with the outside hand, will help the horse to understand what is wanted.

(c) Head tilting, caused by crossing the inside hand over the neck.
4. Re-demonstrate as required, at walk and trot.
5. Further practice. Generally better at trot, once horse and rider have grasped the principle of the exercise, because there is more impulsion and the rhythm is more marked and easier to feel.
6. Prove the lesson.

Finish with some lengthening or canter work, to ensure that forward movement is retained.

The next lesson could be on a large circle in the open, well spaced out. The ride all reduce the circle together until told to 'Hold it', then increase again on command. The exercise may be done in sitting trot, and alternated with rising trot on a long rein for relaxation.

Stress the importance of methodical working in and relaxation during training for horse and rider. Some people can become too intense and demanding at this stage for the good of either party!

DOUBLE BRIDLE

Reference: *Manual No 2*, pages 50–51 and 265–269.

Riders should first study the action and fitting of a double bridle — or pelham — and should practise riding with double reins on a snaffle. Anybody who wishes to use any form of curb bit for showing or any other purpose must be taught to understand how to use it, and to treat it with respect.

CHANGING HORSES

Reference: *Manual No 2*, pages 54–55.

This should now be encouraged, both on the flat and jumping, governed by considerations of safety. It should be followed by discussion of the horses' good points, problems and training requirements.

Experience of riding horses of different types and levels of training is a necessity for B riders.

JUMPING

The emphasis should be on further development of the strength and independence of the rider's seat, on style and contact, on the connection between dressage and jumping, and on knowledge and control of the horse's stride. The horse should maintain rhythm and bend in his jumping, and be willing to lengthen or shorten the stride when asked.

Useful exercises are:

1. *Manual No 2*, page 36, exercise 4, smaller circles on the circumference of a big circle, is splendid for working-in, improving balance and stride control. Jumping position should be used, at trot or canter, and it can be done by a small ride, provided they are widely spaced and the main circle is very large.

140

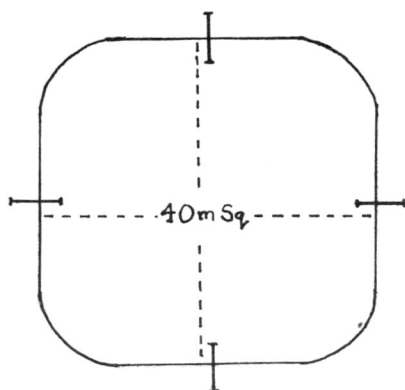

Left: Four fences on a 40m square.

Below: Right-angle exercise: (**A**) 14m, 3 strides, approach and depart straight. (**B**) Allows for longer stride or greener horse. (**C**) 10.3m approx — 2 strides, approach and depart slight angle. (**D**) Not allowed — unnecessary if properly sited.

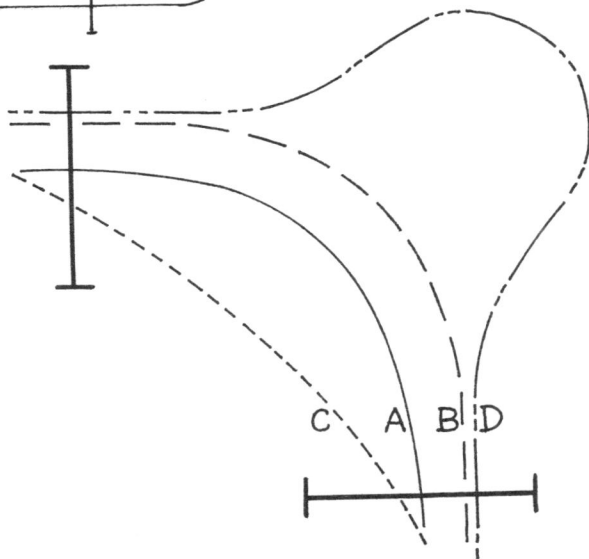

2. Trotting poles, circling alternately left and right. The horse is carefully placed and asked to canter as he circles away, brought back to trot on the approach to the poles.

3. Four fences on a 40m (132ft) square. Riders must maintain rhythm and make a straight approach to each fence.

4. The gymnastic exercise on page 69, *Manual No 2*, gradually developed. Ask the rider to count the strides out loud as he goes through the exercise. This may also be done in combinations.

5. Jumping at an angle — may be practised over a single fence on a figure of eight. Be very particular about canter leads.

6. Jumping two fences at right angles. Show how to measure for two strides, one stride or a bounce, and then let each member attempt to ride it in these three different ways.

7. Jumping one or two fences at a strong canter — excellent after the foregoing, more restricted, exercises.

Practice should continue over both show-jumping and cross-country courses, which may become progressively more demanding as to 'track' and size of fences.

GAMES

At this stage, many members may enjoy helping with games for junior riders, acting as stewards or non-riding team captains, and later as organisers, rather than taking part themselves. Some may display considerable inventive powers in devising new games or musical/activity rides. This should be encouraged to the full.

At the same time, there should be opportunities for those who still wish to participate, and advice and assistance should be available in this department, as in all others.

KNOWLEDGE OF PONY CLUB

Members should now have a clear appreciation of the objects and general structure of the Pony Club movement. They should be prepared to take their share of responsibility, and be encouraged and expected to assist in every possible way. At the same time, they have the right to expect help and instruction for themselves.

HORSE MANAGEMENT

Outside visits and speakers are invaluable for variety at this stage, e.g., talk by vet, visit to saddler, farrier or good stables. Members could offer to help in stables during holidays to gain first-hand experience, which is essential for B Certificate candidates.

SPECIMEN LESSON

Conformation — Stage Pre-B3
Reference: *Manual No 2*, pages 130–140.
As with all wide subjects, this one must be broken down into digestible portions. This lesson allows for class involvement without undue emphasis on any one horse.

Requirements: ride's horses, unsaddled, tied up on tying rail, with sufficient space to get between them easily. All members should bring a tape measure, or even a length of string.

Discuss 'General Impression, Balance and Proportion', on page

131, and the measurements on page 130, *Manual No 2.*

Each member then measures their own horse, with special reference to the 'A' lines. Discuss how the equality of these lines enhances the horse's appearance, balance and working capability, and how irregularities are likely to relate to these factors and/or known training problems.

The next lesson could be on movement, concentrating on how to run a horse up in hand to observe his action, what is meant by a straight mover, and how faults in action are likely to affect the horse's usefulness for various purposes.

Conformation is a subject that lends itself well to the five-minute talk on a specific point — e.g., good and not-so-good feet, knees, hocks, shoulders, etc. If you use a horse to show the 'not-so-good', be sure to point out some other, good aspect of his conformation.

6
TEACHING OLDER AND ASSOCIATE MEMBERS TOWARDS A & H CERTIFICATES

A Pony Club A Certificate holder, now successful at international level.

These members are in a unique position in our organisation. Apart from being the smallest group, many of them are becoming instructors and committee members, valuable in the running of their clubs and branches. Most are also active and often very competitive riders, much in need of help for themselves. A give-and-take basis is most important.

Some who have passed B level may feel that the average Pony Club rally has little to offer. Despite this, they are bound to attend a set number of rallies to qualify for area trials, inter-Pacific and A and H tests.

Careful thought should be given to the best way of integrating these important members into the Pony Club system, if their interest is to be maintained.

It must first be realised that they are not children. For the most part, they are involved in tertiary education or employment situations. It is an age when time is limited and interests are many. Often what is needed, just as much as technical instruction, is an opportunity for discussion, to sort out their priorities and aspirations in riding and Pony Club.

Many older members will not want to go beyond, or even as far as, B level. They may come to Pony Club for the social side, as a relaxation in their busy lives, because they love horses and riding and want to keep in touch. They often enjoy hunting, showing, horse trials and jumping at novice level, as well as games, treks and other less technical aspects of riding. They should know that help and encouragement are available.

It may be best if the 'round-about-B' people work with those who are aiming for A. Rides in any case are likely to be small, and it is not difficult to work in the open with people of different levels of ability but similar age-group. Riders can work independently in the school, and will also be doing individual exercises. A's can demonstrate B work, and the two groups can be paired off for mutual assistance and checking on basics.

If the B's express a desire to try more advanced movements such as lateral work and counter canter, provided their horses are reasonably steady, let them. They will probably enjoy it immensely, and enthusiasm may well build up.

Many of these people will enjoy teaching younger members, organising and taking games, helping in taking rides out and treks — things which will involve them in the life of their club without being too demanding in time, mental fatigue or regular attendance.

Anybody interested in instructing should first be asked to assist an experienced instructor, and, if considered suitable, should then be put forward to attend a basic instructors' course. However keen, or good a rider, they should *never* be put in front of a class with no training to prepare them. Many potentially excellent instructors are lost forever in this way.

H Certificate is the ideal goal for members who are interested in learning more about horses, their conformation, care and management, rather than the advanced riding techniques required for A Certificate. The particular sphere of H Certificate holders in Pony Club will be in teaching horse management, coaching candidates for this aspect of tests, advising on conditioning and fitness, helping to organise Pony Club grazing and the care of horses on camps and treks.

A Certificate. A minute proportion of Pony Club members throughout the world reaches A standard. They are the real riding enthusiasts. Many have hopes of a career with horses, either as instructors or as competitive riders, and some achieve the highest levels. Most of the Olympic riders in the English-speaking countries started in Pony Club.

Pony Club is intensely proud of these members, who are an example and an incentive to all the members in their clubs. Every effort must be made to provide the instruction that they need.

CRITERIA FOR INSTRUCTORS

Similiar to those for B Certificate, but with greater knowledge and understanding of the more advanced requirements for A and H, gained by ongoing study and experience.

A and/or H Certificate course, or Association course at this level, with National Instructors.

Attendance as an observer at A/H examinations. Instructors who are training candidates for these tests may apply to the Association to attend an examination, but not where their own pupils are candidates.

Observers gain a real insight into the conduct and standard of tests, as they can watch and listen-in to all sections, and are encouraged to ask questions and discuss the results with the examiners afterwards.

INSTRUCTOR'S OBJECTIVES

1. Understanding.

(a) Of the initial handling of a young horse, and of the groundwork and further training required to bring him to the standard of elementary dressage and novice jumping and eventing, as well as being a well-mannered and pleasant ride.

(b) Of riders' own and their horses' strengths and weaknesses, of what they are achieving and the work needed for improvement.

(c) Of the varying temperaments and problems of different horses, and how to ride and handle them so that they will give willingly of their best.

(d) Of the relationship between performance and horse management — feeding, exercise, shoeing, etc.

(e) Of the basic anatomy of the horse, and how conformation can affect his soundness and suitability for certain types of work.

(f) Of the Pony Club movement and their place in it.

2. Technique.

(a) Further improvement in the rider's position, which should be supple and stylish, enabling aids to be applied with sublety and accurate timing. The rider's strength will be less in evidence than at B level, but available as and when needed. Confidence, style and polish are the key words, both on the flat and over fences.

(b) To encourage/assist pupils to acquire practical familiarity with all the procedures involved in stabling, conditioning, clipping and trimming, basic veterinary care and lunging.

Problems

1. Lack of instructors at this level, and sometimes poor utilisation of those who are, or could be, available.

Any instructor who teaches regularly at B level can be of assistance in the general work towards A and H, and there may be capable people in the district who could well help with more specialised aspects, even if they do not have time to commit themselves to regular attendance at rallies.

It may sometimes be helpful to call on professional assistance, perhaps sponsored by the club. In this case, the club instructor should try to be present to hear the comments on each rider, so that training may continue along the same lines.

All instructors, whether professional or amateur, must be thoroughly imbued with Pony Club ideals, principles and methods. They should never lose sight of the fact that the Pony Club's aim is to give its older members a good grounding in a wide range of subjects on conventional lines. While other ideas and methods should be discussed, and may sometimes be beneficial in certain cases, too much emphasis on advanced show-jumping or even dressage techniques can mitigate against the all-round development of the Pony Club rider. This must be based on one coherent system, as set out in these manuals.

2. The fact that the older, more advanced members are so widely scattered. Many branches and some clubs will have neither pupils nor instructors at A or H level.

Training may have to be organised on an area basis. District Commissioners and Chief Instructors might get together to discuss and appoint the most suitable people as trainers. This would cut down on travelling, host clubs would have the opportunity to see the 'tops' in their area, and it would stimulate interest in the higher tests and support for the candidates. At the same time, candidates must be encouraged to get together and help themselves, on the lines suggested in *Manual No 2*, Chapter 21.

Attendance as a 'guinea pig' at an Association course, and as a participant on other instructors' courses, would also be beneficial.

3. Just occasionally, a 'know-it-all' attitude on the part of riders, or a feeling that none of their local instructors is good enough to help them.

Those who take these attitudes should realise that *everybody* develops faults which are often impossible to identify oneself, when riding, but may be quite clear to any knowledgeable person. Video can be helpful to both parties.

4. The Associate member working towards A or H who is also the Head Instructor. No problem, provided the committee makes sure that these people get whatever assistance and support they need. A point that is often overlooked.

TEACHING DRESSAGE — STAGES PRE-A1 AND 2

These riders should already have good foundations, be developing the ability to analyse results and to work to a logical programme. They should understand the principles of progressive training and how to go about commencing new movements.

The instructor must keep the basics firmly in mind. It is so easy for the rider to lose sight of them, in the excitement of attempting more and more new things. Straightness and impulsion are particularly at risk. Remember to check from in front and behind, as well as from the side.

Rhythm must also be watched. Trot or canter round the school with large circles and other simple movements help to relax and maintain the rhythm, between the more difficult exercises. Riding to music is excellent. Suggest that each rider devises their own freestyle to music, including only movements in which they can keep the rhythm. Other movements may be added as they improve.

Emphasise that dressage movements are not circus tricks, and help riders to work out which movements would most benefit their own horse.

For example, if the horse is stiff in his back, use circles of different sizes, and decrease and increase of circle, leading up to shoulder-in, probably the best suppling and 'lightening' exercise of all.

If he is heavy and on the forehand, demi-pirouettes, canter from walk and other transitions would help, as well as shoulder-in.

For stiff shoulders and forehand, use counter canter and shoulder-in.

For general lack of activity and impulsion, lengthening of stride and frequent transitions within the pace.

Remind all of the importance of correct half-halts to prepare and lighten their horses before any movement.

TEACHING LATERAL WORK

Lateral movements are fully covered in *Manual No 2*, pages 158–166. Instructors should study this section thoroughly, if possible in conjunction with a good video or a horse and rider who are able to perform them. Before commencing lateral work with a ride, check that all the horses are calm and steady, 'soft' and responsive in the lead-up exercises of riding in position and increase of circle.

SPECIMEN LESSON

Shoulder-in
Reference: *Manual No 2*, pages 158 and 162–164.
Explain objects. Watch demonstration or video. If neither available, draw on blackboard, showing approach, positioning of horse (as in picture on page 158, *Manual No 2*) and aids. Stress that rider must sit straight and use the inside leg actively but lightly. Hands must allow the horse to move along the track, but not off it.

Work-in should include increase of circle and possibly leg yielding.

Start the shoulder-in at walk, from a 10–12m circle in the corner of the school, emphasising the exact moment to apply the half-halt and almost simultaneously ask the horse to move away from the inside leg. A few steps, praise and circle away.

The instructor should stand in or close to the track, near the half marker. Look for:

1. The horse moving freely along the track, his forehand slightly in, with a comfortable bend throughout. His hind feet should point straight along the track. (If they are angled, it implies that he is leg yielding, rather than doing shoulder-in.) He should be on three tracks, the outside foreleg in front of the inside hind.

2. The straightness and relaxation of the rider. (Forcing with the inside leg causes the hip to collapse, a very common fault in the early stages. Better to emphasise the leg with light taps of the dressage whip, if necessary.)

3. The co-ordination of leg and hand aids, with the emphasis on the horse moving away from the inside leg to the outside hand.

For common faults and their possible causes, see *Manual No 2*, page 164.

The rhythm may vary a little as horse and rider find their way.

With those who have difficulty, try reverting to the increase of circle on approaching the side of the school, then continuing down the long side for a few steps.

Continue with shoulder-in at walk until the rider is sure of the aids and the horse understands what is required. Trot on in between times, and finish with some lengthening to maintain impulsion.

In trot, it is essential that the rider can sit softly. At this stage the use of back and seat aids is minimal.

When riders and horses are familiar with the movement, it may sometimes be carried out at a steady rising trot in the open with great benefit.

Later on, when the horse is capable of more collection, the back and seat aids play a greater part. If they are used too soon, the rider is inclined to stiffen and become crooked, making it impossible for the horse to remain soft.

While shoulder-in is one of the most valuable suppling exercises for horses, it is also the hardest that the rider has had to master to date. A positive approach and every encouragement on the part of the instructor can do much to mitigate any sense of frustration which may otherwise develop in the early stages.

CHANGING HORSES

This should now be encouraged frequently, but not when the horses are learning new movements. This could result in all-round confusion. The objects are for riders to learn to differentiate between the sensitivity of different horses, to assess their state of training and the work required for improvement.

DOUBLE BRIDLE

When horses are ready for it, some work in a double bridle should be encouraged, so that riders may become more expert in its use.

LUNGING THE RIDER

Reference: *Manual No 2*, pages 144–146.

Lunging, properly conducted and adapted to individual fitness and ability, is beneficial to riders at all levels, but it is not often feasible for more junior rides at Pony Club, because of the one-to-one relationship it requires, and the lack of suitable horses and facilities.

However, at A level, riders should be encouraged to train their horses to lunge, for the reasons given in *Manual No 2*, page 254. (For teaching pupils to lunge their horses, see page 154.) A candidates will then be able to lunge each other, both during lessons with an instructor and for practice among themselves.

From the instructor's point of view, it is an advantage to have someone else lunging the horse, as it enables you to give your undivided attention to the rider, and to check the all-important straightness from outside the circle.

Work on the lunge is unequalled for the training of A riders. It develops the suppleness, strength and elegance of position, combined with accurate muscle control, necessary at this standard.

The aim should be to achieve a balanced and supple seat, with the hands in riding position, at all paces and through transitions.

Care should be taken to select exercises which will be most helpful for individual riders. Any physical disability must be borne in mind, so that suitable exercises may be ascertained. Always specify the number of repetitions to be done, or the number of circuits. Exercises must be done slowly and smoothly, in rhythm with the horse's movement, and with no jerks. The rider must try to use only the muscles involved in the exercise and to keep everything else relaxed and still.

There are countless exercises that may be done on the lunge. The following is a selection to supple and strengthen all parts of the body, and to improve the rider's balance.

For suppling and relaxing neck and jaw
1. Look right, look left, look up, look down, tip right ear towards right shoulder, left ear towards left shoulder. All very gently.
2. Make a horizontal figure of eight (sign of infinity) with the nose.

For the arms and hands
1. Hand and arm stretched forward, towards the bit, separately and together — i.e., right forward, left forward, both forward. Body must remain upright.
2. Hands raised and lowered, as above. If the elbow is particularly stiff, the hand may be brought up until the thumb touches the shoulder.

Both these exercises are excellent for co-ordination.
3. Wrist circling, both ways, and wrist shaking, with relaxed fingers.

Shoulder and trunk exercises
1. Arms out to either side, at shoulder height. Good for checking straightness and balance.
2. Arms as above, body turning from side to side, looking back over the horse's tail. Arms must stay up and in a straight line
3. Shoulder shrugging, together and separately, with arms down to

the sides, or hands on hips. At the end of the exercise, emphasise and hold the good, open position of the shoulders.

4. Elbows bent, at shoulder height, finger-tips touching, palms down. Pull elbows back quietly twice, and on the third beat open arms right out to either side. Arms must remain at shoulder height throughout, and head must not poke forward.

5. Arm circling. Arms, separately, together, or following one another, windmill fashion. See illustration, page 107.

6. Toe touching, from arms hanging down position. Down slowly to the same toe, up more quickly.

To open the hips and get seat bones closer to the saddle

Sitting in the lowest part of the saddle, holding the pommel, stretch the legs downwards and the body upwards. Lift both legs from the hip, away from the saddle, returning the thigh to the saddle flap with the knee well down and the inner thigh muscles lying as flat as possible. This exercise can be strenuous for the unfit, and can cause painful cramps if overdone, but, used correctly, it is very valuable.

Leg exercises

To supple the knees and increase the independence of the lower leg:

1. Leg swinging alternately from the knee — as one goes forward the other goes back. The toe should be down and the whole leg relaxed.

2. Hold ankles alternately and lift, keeping the knee down.

3. To supple the ankles — ankle-turning.

4. To supple all the leg joints. Jockey position — draw legs up to the maximum, body forward. Also helps to stretch the back muscles, and, done in trot, is an excellent balance exercise.

Breathing exercises

1. Sit straight and 'hollow', breathe in slowly and deeply, hold it and stretch up, 'collapse' and round the back while breathing out.

2. As above, starting with arms in front at shoulder height. Raise the arms as you breathe in, lower them as you breathe out.

Remind riders to breathe *out* completely — point out the tendency to hold the breath in moments of stress.

Be constantly on the watch for signs of tension, such as gripping upwards, stiff knee, clenched fingers or jaw. If they appear, bring the horse back to walk, and encourage the rider to shake out any stiffness before proceeding. In trot, revert to the hand on the saddle.

Two of the exercises for B level, 'relaxed' and correct position, and tapping on the thigh in rhythm with the horse's pace, are very useful on the lunge. See *Manual No 2*, pages 29–30.

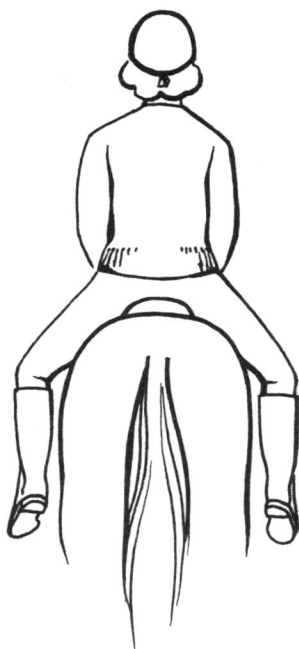

Leg lifting.

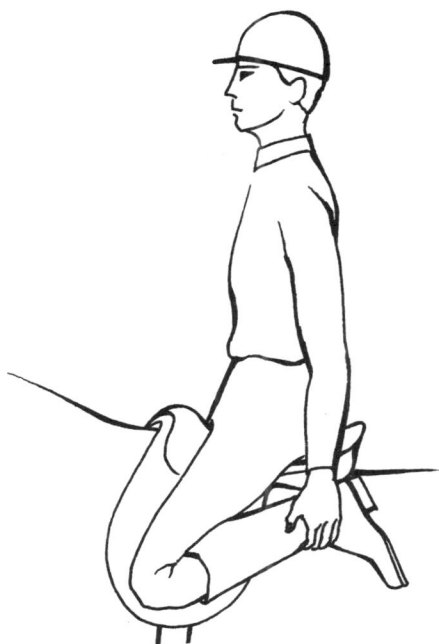

Holding ankles alternately.

This is very intensive work for the rider. Try to keep it as informal and relaxed as possible. If it can be arranged, 'little and often' will bring more benefit than an occasional long session.

JUMPING

The A rider should clearly appreciate the connection between dressage and jumping. He should be able to ride an accurate 'track', keeping the horse in balance and rhythm, with smooth changes of direction and good stride control.

As on the flat, the rider's position must be balanced and supple, strong when necessary. It must be instantly adaptable according to circumstances, without ever being in any way exaggerated. The steadiness of the lower leg, the independence of the hands and the maintenance of contact with hand and leg in front of the fence are of particular importance.

These requirements will only be achieved by constant practice and attention to the basics. Riders at this stage should be fit enough to do some jumping without stirrups, which is especially beneficial for correcting the lower leg position and strengthening the seat.

Riders should be encouraged to:

1. Design and build their own fences and courses (before the lesson). They will then learn from practical experience what will 'ride' and what will not.

2. Understand the use and value of gymnastic exercises in adjusting a horse's stride and improving his jumping style.

3. Experiment with different types of fences in combinations, to see how this affects the optimum distances between them.

4. Above all, gain experience of jumping every possible type of horse over all kinds of obstacles. Every horse, green or experienced, thoroughbred or plebian, will have something to teach the thoughtful rider, and should be discussed and assessed.

Competition, particularly in horse trials with their emphasis on all-round ability of horse and rider, is almost essential to provide the necessary variety of courses and problems, and also to help riders to become accustomed to performing with confidence in public.

YOUNG HORSES

A's must be urged to study the handling and training of young horses right from the beginning. It would be excellent if they could act as assistant in backing, etc., to a good trainer, and later train their own youngster from scratch. For the education and training of young horses, see *Manual No 2*, pages 167–179 and 187–191.

TEACHING LUNGING

Reference: *Manual No 2*, pages 254–260.

This is an essential part of the Pony Club system of training. It is an integral part of the H examination, and, from a practical viewpoint, equally necessary for A's.

Suitable members from C+ onwards may be taught to lunge *provided* the requirements listed below are available. It is definitely not recommended for Pre-C, as it requires authority, technique and sometimes strength which are beyond riders of this age and experience.

The following is a suggested course of lessons:

Lesson 1

Requirements: A well-trained lunge horse, correctly equipped, a suitable enclosure and a capable 'lunger'. Some spare lunge reins and whips.

Beforehand, remind all to bring gloves. Nobody may lunge without them.

Explain the objects of lunging, uses and fitting of equipment. No side-reins at this stage.

Watch the horse working in walk and trot on both reins. Draw attention to the lunger's stance, technique and use of voice.

Halt horse, demonstrate method of holding rein, carrying and handling whip. Class takes it in turns to be 'horse' and 'lunger', practising taking up the rein ready for action, while holding the whip in the other hand.

Watch again — special attention to use of voice, rein and whip on transitions.

Class takes turns to 'lunge' one another, checked by the instructor and assistant. When the rein and whip are held correctly, emphasise clear voice commands.

If the class is small enough and time permits, each may lunge the horse briefly. Prove the lesson.

Finish by rewarding the horse and showing how to lead him away.

Lesson 2

Requirements: One or more lunge horses. One in yard, with equipment laid out close by. Class each fit one item. A class member leads the horse to the lunging area, remembering to shut the gate.

Revise method of holding rein and whip, watch horse(s) working. Possibly repeat lunging one another, but in this lesson everybody must have a chance to lunge a horse. If an enclosed dressage arena is used, one horse can be worked at each end, supervised by the instructor and assistant. Poles may be used for a barrier across the middle.

Re-demonstrate as required. It may be necessary to show how to keep the horse out. Emphasise that contact must be maintained on the rein. It must *never* be allowed to drag on the ground.

Class lunge again. Prove lesson.

Lesson 3

Requirements: As for Lesson 2, with the addition of side-reins.

Tack up horse as before. Introduce side-reins, explain uses and fitting. Stress that they must only be attached to the bit when the horse is actually working.

Class lunge. When horses are worked in, attach side-reins on demonstration horse, watch it being lunged, notice effect of side-reins. Take the opportunity to demonstrate any faults noted in lunging.

Class lunge with side-reins. Prove lesson.

Lesson 4
Requirements: All bring their own horses, tacked up for lunging.

Demonstrate, with one of the class horses, how to start it lunging, led by the owner. See *Manual No 2*, page 172.

Take turns to lunge own horse and lead one another's. Aim to get each to walk on and halt on lunger's command, without intervention by the leader.

Finish on this. Warn not to attempt lunging at home without an enclosure and somebody to lead the horse.

Lesson 5
Requirements: own horses, as before.

Demonstrate, with one of these horses, how to start trot, and how to steady the horse back to walk if he does not obey the voice command. See *Manual No 2*, page 259.

Class work on walk/trot transitions and halts, establishing paces in between.

Cantering on the lunge should not be attempted until the horse is under full control at walk and trot. Then only on good footing, for short periods and on a circle of about 20m. (Moving with the horse, if necessary.)

HORSE MANAGEMENT

Outside experience is absolutely essential for H and A candidates.

Visits to good training or breeding establishments and horse sales are all highly educational. Helping in stables, grooming for eventers or show jumpers, allow for putting theory into practice.

Refer to the manuals and other recommended reading to compare and evaluate the different methods that may be encountered.

It is important that teaching should continue at Pony Club. Apart from practical aspects such as clipping, it is likely that more use will be made of lectures to provide the depth of knowledge required at this level.

SPECIMEN LESSON

Nutritional requirements of horses
Reference: *Manual No 2*, page 199–206.
Requirements: Large wall charts showing the principal feed require-

ments (carbohydrates, proteins, etc.) and the feedstuffs from which they are derived.

A larger presentation of the information given on pages 199–200 of *Manual No 2* will help pupils to absorb it and to fix it in their minds. This could lead on to a discussion of the properties of the various feedstuffs, and of their suitability for different horses in relation to their type, age and work.

At the end of the lesson, hand out a previously prepared, specific case sheet to each member of the class — e.g., three-year-old, recently backed, working about one hour a day; highly strung eventer, eight-year-old, liable to go off feed and run up very quickly; stocky cob, runs to fat, ridden rather irregularly but sometimes for quite long periods; fourteen-year-old hunter, wind suspect. Ask everybody to work out a diet-sheet for their particular case and bring it for discussion at the next rally.

7
EXAMINATIONS

Candidate preparing for lunging at an H examination.
Examiner and Technical Delegate in foreground.

Certificates are an essential part of the Pony Club system, providing incentive and encouragement to learn and improve at all levels. Division of rides is made easier when it is done according to certificates held.

There is provision for an examination approximately every two years throughout a member's time in Pony Club: D at 8 or 9 years, C at 11 or 12, C+ at 13+, B at 15+ and A and H at 17+. Apart from certain exceptions for A and H Certificates (see *Rules and Guidelines for Pony Club Certificates*), the upper age limit for all examinations is 21 years.

None of these tests is compulsory, but Pony Club encourages all members to attain at least C standard, 'to ensure that everybody can ride well enough to establish a safe and happy partnership with their pony, and that all ponies are cared for to a reasonable standard', *Manual No 1*, page 8.

Those who join Pony Club at a later age should require much less time between the earlier tests — in fact, it could be possible for them to take D and C on the same day.

RECORD CARDS

These cards (see page 21) are invaluable to ensure that the syllabus is covered methodically by every member.

If this system is properly used, with sufficient revision at each stage, all the work should be covered in the normal course of events at rallies, and no special coaching needed up to C+. Members should not be put forward for tests until their cards are filled.

Candidates for all tests should take their record cards for perusal by the examiner, if required.

RULES

Since rules for all examinations are subject to revision from time to time, they are printed in a separate publication. This booklet, *Rules and Guidelines for Pony Club Certificates*, is available from the Assocation secretary.

EXAMINERS

For appointment of examiners for all tests, and details of Examiners' Clinics, see *Rules and Guidelines*, as above.

All examiners should be experienced instructors, at least to the level of the test they are examining. They must be thoroughly familiar with the syllabus, and must *never*, in questions or in the work required from the candidate, go beyond or outside this syllabus.

TECHNICAL DELEGATE

The Technical Delegate mediates between all parties, examiners, candidates, parents and instructors. He must have a sound knowledge of the test sheets and the standards required, and the confidence to answer, with complete impartiality, any queries that may arise.

A Technical Delegate must be appointed for all examinations from C+ onwards. See *Rules and Guidelines for Pony Club Certificates*.

CONDUCT OF EXAMINATIONS

A well-conducted examination should be an enjoyable and educational experience for all concerned. However, to many people any form of test is an ordeal. It is up to the examiner (who may also be nervous) to put candidates at ease. You must appear relaxed and confident and carry out the test in such a way that, whatever the outcome, candidates feel that they have had a fair chance to prove their knowledge and ability.

If, during any examination, a potentially dangerous or harmful situation arises through the actions of a candidate, you must not allow it to develop. Act quickly if it is urgent, otherwise question and, if necessary, quietly correct him. Continue the examination, but bear the episode in mind when assessing the candidate.

Examiners should liaise with the District Commissioner or Head Instructor about starting times and programme for the day.

If examining with others, make contact and decide which horse management sections each will take.

Preparation

Work out a format which combines practical work and questions, for both the riding and the horse or pony management sections. Decide which subjects you will go into more deeply, which you will cover with just one or two questions requiring brief answers. Alternate to avoid 'brain drain'. Refer constantly to the Test Sheet and to the appropriate manual when preparing your programme.

Then write down the movements or tasks you intend to ask candidates to perform. Make sure you have the necessary props for feeding, grooming, first aid, etc., or advise the organising club of your requirements.

Write out your questions, with notes on the answers you expect. Allow for pairs or larger groups.

On the day

You will need your notes, a clipboard or notebook, pens and/or pencils, *Manuals, No 1* for D and C, *Nos 1* and *2* for C+ and B, *Rules and Guidelines for Pony Club Certificates*, and, if the weather is wet, a plastic bag to hold these items.

Turnout should be neat and workmanlike. Riding kit or suitable trousers and top, solid footwear.

Arrive at least 45 minutes before starting time, so that you can check layout, jumps, props, etc.

Introductions

The District Commissioner, Technical Delegate or whoever is in charge of the day will introduce candidates and examiners to one another. Name tags all round assist, but be sure to write down each candidate's name, with some means of identification.

Explain briefly how the test is to be run, emphasise that if candidates do not understand what is required they should ask for further explanation.

During inspection ask each candidate their pony's age, how long they have had it, general riding interests. Do not ask the candidate's age — it can be off-putting. (If you really need to know, you can ask the person in charge.)

You *must* put all previous knowledge of any candidate right out of your mind. Never ask about or refer to competitive successes or failures.

All instructions to candidates must be clear, and ample warning given for all commands.

Examinations can be very tiring, especially for younger members. The time allowance for each phase should be adhered to whenever possible.

MARKING AND ASSESSMENT

It is suggested that the following marking system be used for all tests:

A+	Excellent	A−	Very good
B+	Good	B−	Adequate, lowest pass mark
C+	Below standard	C−	Insufficient
D+	Poor	D−	Very poor

Tests are divided into riding and horse/pony management sections, each of which is further divided into phases.

As you examine, write down a brief comment and mark for each part of each phase. When completed, check marks. A preponderance of C+'s or below is an obvious failure, all B's or above, a pass. The most difficult situation is the borderline — some B's, possibly even A's, and some C's. Decide whether the C's were for major or minor points. If in doubt, put down C+/B− and underline the mark you tend to favour. At the end of that section of the test, check marks with your co-examiner(s). If the candidate is C+/B− (borderline) in two or more phases it cannot be a pass.

When assessing, think overall, rather than in petty detail. If there is still doubt, consider:

1. Were the candidate's methods safe?
2. Were the techniques shown acceptable?
3. If the candidate continues on the same lines, will he/she improve?

Examiners should always discuss their findings among themselves, in the presence of the Technical Delegate, before giving the results to the candidates and their supporters.

Summing up and results

Keep it brief and objective. Announce first who has passed and failed, then mention outstandingly good or weak points overall. Comments should be kept fairly general — never give the impression that a candidate failed on one small point. Encourage wherever possible. Even those who have not passed should feel that the test has been worthwhile, and that they have done well in some aspects. They should know just what they must work on to be up to the standard required next time.

Examiners are not obliged to discuss tests after the summing up other than with the District Commissioner, Technical Delegate or club instructors. Written reports will be given only for A and H.

It cannot be emphasised too strongly that candidates, parents and instructors, must accept the examiners' findings without argument. If they have any points to raise, they should approach the Technical Delegate, or, if there is no Technical Delegate, the District Commissioner.

D CERTIFICATE

For Test Sheet, see *Manual No 1*, page 19.
Recommended age, 8 or 9 years. Felt/clip colour, green.

Requirements

Riding section: A small enclosed area, as for D instruction. A 'mounting block' — e.g., a hay bale.

Pony care section: Candidates' own ponies, unsaddled and tied up with halter and rope along a tying rail or fence line. Several small brushes and titbits for the ponies. Saddle and snaffle bridle, for identifying parts.

Notes for examiners

The essence of the D test should be safety, simplicity and fun for the candidates. The examiner must be satisfied that they can carry out the requirements of the test, and that they have an elementary understanding of the correct position and the aids to start, stop and guide the pony. Few questions should be needed to ascertain this.

It is important that each candidate should be asked one or two questions on 'Do's and don'ts for riding on the road'.

Care of the pony must be as practical as possible, with great attention being paid to safe and sympathetic handling of the pony throughout.

It is embarrassing for examiners to be obliged to fail children in this very simple test. It is up to instructors to make sure that members are up to standard before putting them forward.

The format and content of the test must remain the same, whatever the age of the candidate. i.e., older members must not have a harder test.

FORMAT OF THE TEST

Candidates will be taken in groups of two to four. Overall time, 20 to 35 minutes maximum.

Riding section
Explanation. 2 minutes.
Inspection. 3 minutes for two candidates, 6 minutes for four.
Riding. As a suggested programme, each rider could show dismount/ mount. Then, working as a ride, halt one at a time from rear of ride, walk on. Change rein by turning across in single file. Trot front to rear on the other rein. Ask each person simple aids, one question each. Also ask about 'Do's and don'ts on the road'. Finish with some position and activity exercises.

10 to 15 minutes for two candidates, 15 to 20 minutes for four.

Care of the pony section
Each candidate to show, with their own pony, tying-up, brushing over, giving a titbit, leading in hand.

Name simple points of the pony, parts of saddle and bridle.

10 minutes for two candidates, 15 minutes for four.

C CERTIFICATE

For Test Sheet, see *Manual No 1*, pages 42–44.
Recommended age, 11 or 12 years. Felt/clip colour, yellow.

Requirements
Riding section: Space to work in the open, preferably with both flat and undulating ground.

A dressage arena, 40 by 20m, with letters.

Trotting poles and a course of six to eight jumps up to 60cm (2ft), with an easy two-stride double.

If possible, a small ditch and/or a few very small fences on slopes or other cross-country obstacles, close to the other jumps.

Pony care section: Candidates' ponies, unsaddled and tied to a suitable rail or fence.

Own tack, for saddling up and fitting of tack.

Grooming kit.

A few shoes (see *Manual No 1*, page 153).

Samples of hay and basic hard feeds.

Tack cleaning kit.

A table or hay bales on which to lay out props, preferably under cover.

Notes for examiners

Bear in mind that 11- and 12-year-olds, and many inexperienced older riders, often have difficulty in expressing themselves, especially when nervous, even if their knowledge of a subject is quite adequate. Be patient, give candidates time to settle down and to think. Keep questions simple, emphasising knowledge of aids and basic assessment, rather than detailed analysis, of pony's performance.

Care of the pony must be practical and *related to the candidate's own pony.*

FORMAT OF THE TEST

Candidates are best taken in groups of two to four. Time should not exceed 1hr 30min for two, 1hr 45min to 2 hours for four. The following is a suggested timetable:

Riding section, phases 1 to 3. Total time, 45 to 55 minutes.

Phase 1. Explanation, 2 minutes. Inspection, 4 minutes for two candidates, 8 minutes for four. Work in the open on large circle, position, diagonals, paces, including canter. 10 minutes for two to four candidates.

Phase 2. Work in the school, e.g., turns as a ride, 20m circles either end, canter front to rear. Questions on aids, diagonals, etc. 10 minutes for two, 15 minutes for four.

Phase 3. Alter stirrups, check girths, ride up and down hill, open and/or shut gate. Trotting poles, jumping, simple exercise, course, cross-country fences. Questions on Road Code, Pony Club, etc. 15 minutes for two, 20 minutes for four.

Care of the pony section, phases 4 to 7. Total time, 40 to 60 minutes.
  Phase 4. Paddocking, feeding.
  Phase 5. Handling, grooming, shoeing.
  Phase 6. Saddlery and equipment.
  Phase 7. Health and general knowledge (colours, markings).
  10 minutes each phase for two, 15 minutes for four candidates.

C+ CERTIFICATE

For Test Sheet, see *Manual No 2*, pages 15–17.
Minimum age, 13 years. Felt/clip colour, gold.

Requirements
Riding section: As for C Certificate, but with fences up to 75cm (2ft 6in). A one-stride double may be included. A few cross-country fences are most desirable at this level.

Pony management section: Candidates' ponies, tied up as for C. For discussion of shoeing, condition and worming programme.
  Samples of poisonous plants, feedstuffs, etc.
  Grooming, tack cleaning and first-aid kit, farrier's tools.
  Travel boots and bandages. Both are needed, to allow for candidate's choice.
  About six bits in everyday use — to allow for choice of three.

Notes for examiners
This is not intended to be an 'in-depth' examination; the emphasis is on the candidate being 'on the right lines' towards B Certificate. It is halfway between C and B, and should not be examined at B level.
  Candidates should, however, have greater technical knowledge than at C. They should be beginning to develop an ability to analyse, in a realistic manner, their work and the way the pony is going, and understand the objects of, and the aids for, the movements of the test. Where necessary, they must be given the opportunity to improve their performance, after discussion with the examiner.
  The gallop forms an enjoyable part of the C+ test. It shows both spirit and control and should always be included.
  Candidates are not required to change ponies during this test.
  In pony management, candidates must show developing all-round knowledge and ability to care for and condition their ponies.

FORMAT OF THE TEST

Candidates will be examined in twos or threes. Overall time, 1hr 45min to 2 hours maximum. The following is a suggested timetable:

Riding section, phases 1 to 3. Total time, 50 to 60 minutes. Both examiners work together.
  Phase 1. Explanation, inspection, work in the open. 10 minutes.
  Phase 2. Dressage. 20 minutes.
  Phase 3. Jumping. 20 to 30 minutes.

Pony management section, phases 4 to 7. Total time, 50 to 55 minutes. Examiners work separately, taking two sections each.
  Phase 4. Paddock, feeding, exercise, condition.
  Phase 5. Handling, grooming, clipping and shoeing.
  Phase 6. Preparing for travel, saddlery and equipment.
  Phase 7. Health, first-aid.
  10 to 12 minutes for each phase.

B CERTIFICATE

For Test Sheet, see *Manual No 2*, pages 17–21.
Minimum age, 15 years. Felt/clip colour, blue.

Screening. Candidates *must* be screened before being nominated to sit the examination. The screening may be done by holding a mock examination or by assessment and instructional sessions, conducted by the club's B level instructors and/or examiners. If the candidate does not pass this screening, he cannot be nominated to sit the test until further instruction has been received and the required standard attained.

Requirements
Riding section: Space to work in the open.
  Dressage arena, 40 by 20m, with letters.
  Jumping course of six to eight fences, built to a plan supplied by the examiners, or at their suggestion. Maximum height 90cm (3ft).
  Natural fences, six to eight, involving undulating ground, are most desirable, but they must be in close proximity to the other facilities. A cross-country course over several paddocks is not suitable.
  If these fences are not available, the examiners will have to incorporate some 'control' type fences into the jumping course, plus at least one free-riding type of fence, such as a brush.

Changed horse phase. Normally candidates change horses at the examiners' direction. If there are problems of size, or only one candidate, a well-mannered horse, saddled and bridled, should be available.

A quiet horse or pony with a double bridle, adjusted to fit. This horse is only ridden for a few minutes at walk and trot.

Horse management section: A loose box, or failing this, a 'mock-up' where a bed can be put down, bucket and haynet placed. It could be a pen of rails, bales, etc. It is not essential to have a horse inside the box or pen.

Bedding, stable tools, drop skep, haynet, water bucket.

A table, or bales, on which to lay out props.

Props. It is usual for the club to provide standard items like grooming kit and shoeing tools. Other items by arrangement with the examiners.

A quiet horse or pony, used to a loose box if one is being used. For grooming, bandaging, conformation, etc.

As far as possible, all arrangements should be made by the organising club.

Notes for examiners

Keep in mind the first of the objectives for B certificate: 'To become an active and thinking rider, able to assess results.' Candidates should be able to discuss the way their horses are going and their training programme. They should know whether they have achieved specific movements, and if they have not, be able to improve their performance after further discussion.

In jumping, candidates should have a secure, balanced position, with effective contact with hand and leg. They should be able to jump all types of fences at specific paces, and have some basic knowledge of building fences, simple combinations and exercises which will be safe and encouraging and improve their horses' jumping.

When changing horses, safety must be the first consideration. A strong or difficult horse who is under adequate control with his own rider could be dangerous with someone unknown to him. Points to note:

1. The approach to a strange horse, and how the tack is checked, including making sure that the stirrup-irons and leathers are of a suitable size.

2. That the rider checks with the owner prior to mounting with spurs or a dressage whip.

The candidate should ride the horse at all paces, jump a few small, straightforward fences, and be able to assess its way of going.

Do not hesitate to curtail this section of the test if you feel that the rider is having a detrimental effect upon the horse.

Double bridle. In order to retain relativity with other phases, care should be taken to keep within the time allowed. All candidates should fit the curb chain and demonstrate how to hold the reins. This, combined with one or two well-chosen questions, will show whether their knowledge of the fitting, action and use of the bridle is adequate.

Horse management should be as practical as possible. You must see how the candidate goes about handling a horse and carrying out the daily tasks associated with one.

Candidates at this age should be becoming more articulate, but keep questions simple and be prepared to re-phrase them if the candidate seems uncertain.

Throughout the test, candidates must show practical ability and understanding. While some theoretical knowledge is required in both the riding and the horse management sections, they must be able to relate this to the horses they are riding and handling in the test.

FORMAT OF THE TEST

Candidates will be examined in pairs whenever feasible. Possibly in threes when an odd number is involved.

Riding section, phases 1 to 4. Total time, 1hr 15min. Both examiners work together.

Phase 1. Inspection and work in the open. 12 to 15 minutes.

Phase 2. Dressage. 20 minutes.

Phase 3. Jumping, overall. 20 to 30 minutes.

All candidates complete phases 1 to 3. Those who have reached a definite point of failure will only continue the riding section at the discretion of the examiners.

Phase 4. Change horses/ponies. 10 minutes.

Phase 5. Double bridle. 5 minutes per candidate.

Horse management section, phases 6 to 9. Total time, 60 minutes.

Examiners work separately, taking two sections each.

Phase 6. Paddock, feeding, exercise and condition.

Phase 7. Handling, grooming, clipping/trimming, foot and shoeing.

Phase 8. Travel, including bandaging, boots, stabling, saddlery and equipment.

Phase 9. Health, ailments, conformation.

15 minutes each phase.

The above times are maximum for each phase, though when three candidates are examined together the full time will be required.

Total time for two or three candidates, 2hrs to 2hrs 30min.

Candidates failing one part of the test should be allowed to attempt other phases, with the exception of Nos 4 and 5.

The number of candidates in one day should be limited to six, or, with experienced examiners, seven. The following is a suggested timetable:

9.00am	Riding, candidates 1 and 2.
10.15am	Coffee.
10.30am	Horse management, candidates 1, 2, 3 and 4.
11.30am	Sum up first pair, while second pair saddle up.
11.45am	Riding, candidates 3 and 4.
1.00pm	Sum up second pair.
1.15pm	Lunch.
2.00pm	Riding, candidates 5, 6, possibly 7.
3.30pm	Horse management.
4.30pm	Sum up, finish.

If only four or five candidates are being examined, start half an hour later, follow the above suggestions for the first part, but take candidates 3, 4 and possibly 5, for the riding section after lunch.

A and H CERTIFICATES

For Test Sheets, see *Manual No 2*, pages 142–143 and 191–194.

Minimum age, 17 years. Felt/clip colours, A, red. H, purple.

For details of examination dates and venues, and the procedure for nomination of candidates, see *Rules and Guidelines for Pony Club Certificates*.

Horses. Although candidates bring their own horses to A Certificate examinations, extra horses are needed. For H Certificate, all horses have to be supplied.

The Association is extremely grateful to owners who lend horses for use in these examinations. Reasonable transportation costs will be met to bring them to the venue.

A CERTIFICATE

The A Certificate examination consists of two sections, each divided into five phases, as follows:

169

Riding section

Phase 1. Inspection, work in the open.
Phase 2. Dressage.
Phase 3. Jumping own horse.
Phase 4. Jumping other horses.
Phase 5. Green horse.

Horse management section

Phase 6. Stable yard/routine. Horse at grass. Feeding. Conditioning.
Phase 7. Bedding. Grooming. Clipping. Shoeing.
Phase 8. Conformation. Lameness. Travel. Bandaging.
Phase 9. Equipment. Saddlery. Minor Ailments.
Phase 10. Knowledge of Pony Club and other horse-related activities. Training methods.

Requirements

Riding section: Phase 1. Flat ground, adjacent to dressage arena.

Phase 2. Dressage arena, with letters, either 40 by 20m or 60 by 20m. (A long arena may be needed, depending on numbers.)

Phases 3 and 4. Different fences are needed for these two jumping phases. A show-jumping course of about eight fences, including a double. With trotting poles and some spare poles and stands for gymnastic exercises, adjacent to the above.

One or more groups of schooling-type cross-country fences, close together for easy viewing, would be ideal. A cross-country course is not suitable.

The maximum height of all fences is 1.15m (3ft 9in).

Phase 5. Flat ground for work in the open, usually in or close to the jumping area.

Horses. For adequate testing of candidates at this level, it is considered essential that each should ride at least four horses.

One or two green or awkward horses will be needed for Phase 5. These horses must be safe for strangers to ride. They are not required to jump.

Where there is a small number of candidates, one or two additional horses may be needed. These should be at a somewhat more advanced stage of training and capable of jumping up to about 1m (3ft 3in). Good hunter types are usually suitable. Provided they are sound and safe to ride, problems of temperament or behaviour are no deterrent.

Horse management section

Phase 6. Stables. Feed room with various feedstuffs in bins, if available. Otherwise table or bale with samples of hay and hard feed. No horse needed.

Phase 7. Loose box with bedding, preferably straw. Stable tools, drop skep, water bucket. One horse with halter and rope, cover or sheet, haynet for comfort. Table or bale for laying out equipment. Grooming kit, clipping machine with oil and screwdriver, farrier's tools and shoes.

Phase 8. One horse with halter and rope, preferably tied up outside. Covers as needed. Space to run up in hand. One pair of travel bandages with gamgee or wraps. One pair of travel boots. Selection of covers and sheets (need not fit the horse). Knee caps, hock boots, poll and tail guards as available, tail bandage. Hoof pick. Drop skep.

Phase 9. Well-equipped tack room, if available. Otherwise, a loose box with provision for hanging tack, saddle horse. Several saddles of different types. A selection of girths, irons, bits, bridles, nosebands, martingales, lunging gear, as available. Double bridle. One horse — for minor ailments. The horse from one of the previous phases can generally be used.

Phase 10. A room, heated in winter, with seating, for discussion during this phase. This room may also be used for lunch, and for giving out results.

Lunch and morning and afternoon tea for examiners, Technical Delegate, official observers, if any, and local organiser.

FORMAT OF THE TEST

Times depend on the number of candidates. The Chief Examiner will contact the local organiser regarding the timetable and the number of horses required. The following is a broad outline:

Riding section: Phases 1 and 2 — candidates in pairs or in threes, approximately one hour per group. With four to six candidates all complete these two phases first. Phase 3 — all candidates together, approximately 40 minutes. Successful or borderline candidates continue to phases 4 and 5.

Horse management section: Candidates examined in pairs or singly. Approximately 2 hours overall.

H CERTIFICATE

This test is divided into four sections:
1. Stable yard. Horse at grass. Feeding/conditioning. Saddlery.

2. Handling. Bedding. Grooming. Clipping/trimming. Foot and shoeing. Health and condition. Minor ailments and sick nursing.
3. Conformation, ageing, action and movement, buying a horse. Lameness. Travel, clothing, loading on to a float.
4. Fitting of tack. Ride and lead. Put up a rider. Road Code. Lunging.

Requirements
Section 1: Stable yard, loose boxes, feed and tack rooms.
Samples of feed and hay.
Provision for hanging tack, saddle horse. Several saddles, for type and soundness. A selection of girths, irons, bits, bridles, nosebands, martingales, double bridle.
Horse not usually needed.

Section 2: Loose box, with bedding, preferably straw, and stable tools, drop skep or wheelbarrow, water bucket.
Table or bale with grooming kit, clipping machine with oil and screwdriver, farrier's tools and shoes. Medicine chest.
One horse, accustomed to being stabled, with halter and rope, cover or sheet, haynet for comfort.

Section 3: Loose box, yard or tying rail, adjacent to float, with space to run up in hand.
Float, preferably double, attached to towing vehicle. Must have back strap or bar.
Travel boots and bandages with gamgee or wraps, tail bandage. Selection of covers and sheets (need not fit horse). Knee caps, hock boots, poll and tail guards as available, hoof pick.
One horse, with halter and rope, cover or sheet. Must be a guaranteed loader and familiar with the float provided. Drop skep.

Section 4: Adjacent loose boxes or yards, or a tying rail.
Space for ride and lead.
Lunging area, which must be enclosed, nearby.
Hay bale or sheet for lunging equipment. Lunging cavessons, side-reins, lunge reins and whips, brushing boots to fit the horses — different types of above equipment, as available. Drop skep.

Horses. For a half-day's examination, three lunge horses will be required, for a full day, preferably four. These horses may, if suitable, be used for ride and lead, otherwise more will be needed. Different horses may be used in the afternoon.
Lunge horses should be experienced, used to side-reins and have

been lunged recently. Horses for ride and lead should be experienced.

All horses for this section should come with their own tack, including halters, ropes and covers.

Sections 1 and 4 usually run concurrently, as do Sections 2 and 3, therefore the same horses can be used in different sections.

All horses and equipment should be available at least 30 minutes before the start of the examination, to enable the examiners to familiarise themselves with the horses and check the equipment.

Some of the equipment may be supplied by the examiners, by prior arrangement with the Area Representative or local organiser.

Assistance with horses. Since this examination runs to a tight schedule, some assistance with horses is essential. This is a good opportunity for potential candidates to gain invaluable experience. They can help by preparing horses beforehand, being available during the test, and caring for the horses at lunch time and at the end of the day.

A room and catering, as for A Certificate, will also be required.

FORMAT OF THE TEST

Candidates are usually examined in pairs, sometimes singly. Maximum eight in a day. Time — Sections 1 and 4, 50 minutes each, Sections 2 and 3, 40 minutes each. Total 3 hours.

Candidates, organisers and examiners will receive a timetable from the Association secretary.

8
COMPETITIONS

Team competitions are preferable to individual ones.
Teams at an inter-club gymkhana.

Competition can provide challenge, fun and education for all ages and standards, but, as mentioned in Chapter 1, it must never be allowed to predominate to the extent that there is no time for regular rallies and other activities. Events held must be in accordance with Pony Club principles, and must relate to what is taught at rallies.

The following points should be borne in mind:

1. The programme must be carefully planned beforehand and well run on the day, to avoid long delays and late finishes. Parents should be involved at all stages.

2. At all Pony Club events constant attention must be paid to the proper care of the ponies. Reminders over the public address system or by instructors or stewards should be given whenever necessary in such matters as incorrect tying-up, people galloping about or just sitting around on ponies between events, girths not slackened or stirrups not run up. Whenever possible, there should be a lunch interval during which ponies can be watered, fed and rested.

3. For best rider and show classes and for jumping (other than FEI) it is *essential* to choose judges who are familiar with Pony Club methods and with current ideas on riding and training.

Show classes

'Best Pony Club Mount' (possibly including one or two small jumps and a gallop for intermediate and senior riders) or 'Best Paced and Mannered' are recommended rather than straight show classes. It is strongly advised that snaffles only be allowed for all ponies under 127.5cm and for all novice and maiden ponies and horses. Double bridles or pelhams may be allowed for open classes. Junior and novice riders should not wear spurs.

Rings must be large enough for competitors to spread out. If numbers are very large, allow time to judge in relays, seeding out the best three or four in each section for final judging.

Turnout classes should emphasise the cleanliness and neatness of the pony and rider and the safety, soundness and cleanliness of the tack, not its newness or value. All grooming, plaiting and tack cleaning *must* be the rider's own work, except for the very young, who must have made some visible effort.

Dressage

It is essential to choose tests to suit the age and standard of the competitors. The booklets *Junior Riding Tests* and *Teams, Dressage Championships* are available from the Association secretary, and other tests may be obtained from the NZ Horse Society.

Gymkhanas

It is suggested that the rules set out in the booklet *The Pony Club Mounted Games* should be used at club and branch level. Note that whips and spurs are not allowed, and only snaffle bits may be used.

A number of excellent team events — always preferable to individual ones — will be found in this booklet. Avoid anything which involves pulling ponies about unnecessarily — e.g., 'turning' (making a complete turn round each bending pole) or reining back.

Show jumping

Jumping under FEI rules — the most widely used code for jumping competitions, offering great variety of events and courses, can be suitable for all age groups, provided that the height of fences and the 'track' is appropriate to the grade. On no account should juniors jump off against the clock.

'Clear round' jumping, where all who achieve a faultless round receive a certificate stating the maximum height of the fences, is an excellent system for a practice competition day.

American show hunter jumping makes use of a flowing type of course, with fences as natural-looking as possible. It is judged under a set code, with no jump-off, and heights are strictly regulated for each grade. The emphasis is on style throughout the round.

It should have a wide appeal for Pony Club, because any pony/horse of average ability can win if the rider is prepared to put the work in. It is an excellent preparation for eventing or FEI jumping.

'Round the ring' jumping is less suited to modern training requirements, as the lines of fences without change of direction are inclined to make ponies 'hot' and excitable in all their jumping. If it is used, beware of overlong distances in combinations, which further encourage speed and flat jumping.

All courses, under whatever code, must be suitable for the standard of the competitors, producing a fair proportion of clear rounds and a minimum of falls or eliminations. Much thought and care is needed in planning and building courses for juniors — their first experiences are of the utmost importance.

Horse trials
There are four grades of horse trials in Pony Club; Introductory, Pre-training, Training and Open, including area trials and championships. Details of rules, dressage tests, dimensions of fences and speeds for cross-country and show jumping will be found in the current Pony Club *Horse Trials Rule Book*.

Tetrathlon
A four-phase competition, involving riding, running, swimming and shooting. Excellent for the all-rounders, who are less interested in technical equestrian events. Equally popular with boys and girls.

The riding phase comprises a straightforward cross-country course, to be ridden on an unknown horse. Assistance from kindred organisations will be needed for the other phases.

Some clubs have held very successful tetrathlons involving, say, a dressage test, a jumping round (show or cross-country), a long-distance ride of about 10km (6 miles) for juniors and several gymkhana events — members riding their own ponies. This offers obvious scope for adaptation for different age-groups, and to make use of available facilities.

TRAINING FOR COMPETITIONS

Well beforehand, discuss the condition of the ponies and their fitness for the type of competition. Suggest training and feeding programmes for each pony.

Ensure that each member knows exactly what is entailed in each competition, what saddlery is allowed and what turnout is required.

Explain the rules — all must be conversant with them and must understand that they have to be obeyed.

Allow some time for practice at rallies at the start of the season. Inspection could feature correct turnout and give an opportunity to check any necessary tack repairs and the ponies' shoeing, so that they can be attended to in time.

Discuss what to take for pony and rider, and the care of the pony on the day. Emphasise the importance of good manners — politeness to judges and officials, accepting judges' decisions in a sporting spirit, presenting yourself tidily for prize-givings, returning numbers promptly to the organisers, and *thanking them* at the end of the day.

Remind members to keep their float area tidy and clean it up thoroughly before leaving, never to drop litter and to collect all their belongings.

Whenever possible, attend competitions at which your pupils are competing, and make it plain that you are available to help if asked. It gives you an opportunity to see how they perform in public, and your moral support and practical assistance (course-walking, etc.) will be appreciated. Don't be too critical on the day, but first-hand knowledge of what went on will enable you to be much more helpful afterwards.

GYMKHANA EVENTS

Requirements: Bending poles, flags, buckets, sacks, etc., as needed for the games and races being held.

Reference: *Manual No 1*, pages 96–97, and *Mounted Games and Gymkhanas.*

RING EVENTS

Requirements: A large enough ring for the number taking part — possibly marked out with flags.

Reference: *Manual No 1*, pages 97–99.

Remind participants of the importance of spotless turnout, grooming and condition of pony. No martingales, breastplates, boots, bandages. Check what bits are allowed.

Work round the ring, stand in centre. Emphasise that riders must spread out in single file — the judge can't assess ponies he can't see. Work on both reins, all paces. The exercises on the large circle are all valuable, and should be familiar to the ride.

For Juniors and novices, make sure that all ponies are under control when cantering together. Start when well worked in, in sections or front to rear, if necessary. Stress that ponies must canter on either leg. Check that everybody can tell, without looking down, whether the pony *is* on the correct leg. Help those who have problems. Point out that, if wrong, the rider must bring the pony back to trot and try to correct it. This at least shows that the rider is aware of the fault!

Emphasise the importance of listening carefully to the steward's commands.

Call in and line-up. Explain that the judge calls people in the approximate order in which he expects to place them. The less likely ones will be in the back row. With a big class, the judge may not have time to speak to all these people individually. Don't be too disappointed if you are one of these. Try to find out what was wrong and do better next time, but remember that some very good ponies just don't have the conformation to win show classes. (Hence the preference for classes where training counts for more than conformation.)

Practise individual shows. Encourage riders to devise their own — whatever they feel the pony does best and they are happy doing. As much variety as possible, but remind riders that it is better to do simple things well than complicated ones badly.

Practise figure of eight, often asked for by judges. Have two markers in the centre to help riders to keep their bearings, and ride two even circles. Without this training, riders tend to wander all over the paddock. In canter, change through trot in the centre.

For the more experienced. These riders should be familiar with the foregoing, and be developing a higher standard of showmanship. If considered capable of using a double bridle or pelham, they must be taught how to fit and use it (emphasise only for showing). See *Manual No 2*, pages 50–51 and 265–269.

Remind riders at this stage that they must really gallop on, if asked to do so in the ring. Practise this.

For older members, once they are familiar with the procedure, it is valuable experience and good fun to take turns in acting as steward and judge. Especially useful for those who are learning about conformation and movement.

Best rider classes. Point out that general turnout and the pony's way of going are most important — if it goes badly, the rider may well be at fault. Numbers are often too large for thorough judging, and even the best riders can sometimes be overlooked if unlucky.

Tell riders to remember diagonals and correct canter leads, avoid stiffness and try, above all, to present a picture of harmony and partnership between pony and rider. Older riders may be asked to change horses — this may be practised in training.

DRESSAGE TESTS

Requirement: 40 by 20m dressage arena, with letters.
Reference: *Manual No 1*, pages 102–108.

Junior and novice riders. Begin with a Pony Club Junior Riding Test or one of the simpler Preliminaries. Make sure that the individual movements have been practised in class and are familiar to all.

During a rest period in the school, give out test sheets, point out briefly the 'track' of the test, emphasising that work has been done on all these movements.

Lesson 1. If possible, have a competent older rider to demonstrate the test. Park 'judge's' car at C, with ride lined up behind. Show how to ride round outside the arena while awaiting the bell, how to circle to the pony's best side and enter at A, making a straight approach to the centre line. Comment during the test, especially on good points and the preparation needed for transitions and changes of direction. Explain how important it is to learn the test, so that you know what comes next and can prepare in time. Also to look as relaxed and happy as possible — smile at the judge on salutes. Show how to leave the arena.

Have each member of the ride practise the entry, halt and salute and the next movement of the test. Ask everyone to try to learn the test before the next rally. Suggest ways of doing this — on foot, in a miniature arena, or by drawing an arena on paper and filling in the movements. Not by doing it over and over again on the pony.

Lesson 2. Work-in in the school by practising movements from the test, with ponies as widely spaced as possible.

Then with a large ride, work on three or four movements at a time, in sections, right through the test. This does not allow for accurate transitions at markers, but it does give an opportunity to perfect the shape of circles, for example. With a small ride, the movements can be ridden individually.

Explain the divisions of the test, and how each movement is marked separately, so that a mistake or a course error is not a total disaster. Suggest reading *Manual No 1*, pages 102–108

Lesson 3. Work-in as before. Unless the ride is very small, try to arrange to have an assistant who can keep the others occupied on basic paces and transitions outside the school, while you take each rider through the test individually. This is very important as a confidence booster.

Discuss the 'assessments' and how they are marked. Show a filled-in judging sheet, and explain how important it is to collect this after the test. The judge's comments will help them to improve their performances.

Remind riders to arrive early for the test, to allow time to get ready and work-in calmly. Discuss work-in period needed for each pony. Check all know the rules for course errors, etc.

More experienced riders will be familiar with the procedure, but must receive help as needed with any particular aspects of the test, and must also have the opportunity to run through it with their instructor.

SHOW JUMPING

Requirements: A course of fences suited to the standard. Start and finish flags. Bell.

Reference: *Manual No 1*, pages 99–102, and *Manual No 2*, pages 72–73.

Junior and novice riders, Post-D to C standard. Before entering any jumping event, riders must be capable of maintaining a steady pace round a simple, flowing course, including an easy two-stride double, with fences up to about 45cm (1ft 6in).

Their first competitive course at Pony Club must not exceed this height or degree of difficulty, so training becomes a question of polishing existing skills, and teaching the essential rules and procedure in the ring.

Arrange for horse-holders, so that you can walk the course on foot with the ride. Make sure everyone knows:
1. Which way to circle before going through the starting flags.
2. The exact track they should follow.
3. How to leave the arena after going through the finish flags.

Explain the rules re starting bell, start and finish flags, what to do in the event of a refusal at a single fence or at a combination.

Work-in in jumping position, see page 86. If the ponies are excitable, working together on a big circle, dividing them into sections on several smaller circles may be helpful.

Then practise over a single fence for position, contact, maintaining balance and impulsion on the approach and on the getaway. Also over any new or unusual fences, which you think could cause problems.

Each rider then comes out individually, canters on a circle while awaiting the bell, rides the course and leaves the ring correctly, rewarding the pony for good work. The next rider should be working quietly on a circle, preparing for his turn. The rest of the ride lined up watching and commenting on the accuracy and style with which the course is ridden, and 'judging' the faults, if any.

Those who did not have clear rounds jump the same course again, after discussion with the instructor as to how their performance could be improved. Those who went clear may have fences raised for a 'jump-off', at the instructor's discretion. Explain the rules for this, and how it usually takes place over a shortened course. It must not be judged on time at this stage.

As each rider 'finishes on a good note' he should dismount, run up stirrups and slacken girths, and ponies should be led away at the end of the lesson. Suggest that all read *Manual No 1*, pages 99–102.

Several lessons on these lines may be needed before you can be satisfied that everyone is confident and knows what they are doing.

Intermediate riders, C to B. As riders progress they should be taught at rallies, to pace out combinations, to decide whether the distance will be normal, long or short for their particular mount, and to ride accordingly.

Fences will be gradually increased in height and difficulty. Riders should be taught how to approach different types of spread and upright fences, and how to cope with jumps with a short approach or a turn soon after landing, and to jump at an angle.

All this will require greater stride control, and emphasises the value of dressage to improve a jumper's balance, suppleness and responsiveness. Riders should read *Manual No 2*, pages 72–73 and 81–82.

The exercises given on page 141 are all invaluable for competitive riders.

If pony and rider are given time to develop in the all-round context of Pony Club training, few problems should arise. These usually occur when jumping is allowed to predominate, with insufficient attention to basic principles. Big fences must not be attempted, particularly at speed, until the partnership is fully established.

Inexperienced riders on graded ponies, most of which are keen at the very least, can present some of the biggest problems for instructors. It is essential to get parental co-operation in a 'go-slow' policy in all senses, discouraging both height and speed until experience is gained and the pony under control.

Once they can ride an accurate track at a steady pace with some degree of stride control, riders may be taught how to ride against the clock. Emphasise that fast times are made by taking the shortest possible route at which balance and rhythm can be maintained and jumping at an angle where this will save time. A flat-out gallop will only carry them out wider on turns.

Walk and discuss the course thoroughly, then time each rider over it. Discuss with those who took longer why this was, and let them try again if the pony is not too excited. Fences for this should be big enough to make the ponies pay attention and work — scampering round over very tiny obstacles *will* make them careless and rattle-headed.

On no account must ponies or riders be overfaced — not everyone wants to jump bigger fences. Never be afraid to lower them when sorting out problems.

Pair or team competitions, such as the various relay or jigsaw events, under Table A rather than Table C (speed) conditions, provide excellent practice for riders at intermediate level. A six-bar is always popular and a good gymnastic exercise into the bargain. If increasing heights are used for each obstacle, make sure the first one is not too big! The similar 'obstacles-in-line', with different types of fences, is a useful variation.

Advanced riders, B level and beyond. Those who have graded (possibly A grade) ponies and horses and are establishing successful partnerships with them, still need training. They may not have fences at home, and naturally want to practise over a course at Pony Club, particularly at the start of the season.

Attention must be drawn to the importance of conditioning to ensure fitness for jumping at this level, and of introducing gymnastic exercises gradually before attempting a full course of fences. Courses must be built to suit the grade, with an absolute maximum of 1.2m (4ft) for ponies. This is quite enough for most horses.

Instructors need to have a sound knowledge of show-jumping technique. Their role is to improve the rider's style and correct any faults before they become ingrained. It must always be remembered that show jumping in the higher grades depends largely on the rider's eye and his confidence in seeing his horse's stride, and this can easily be upset by carping criticism. Think twice before making alterations for purely theoretical reasons when good results are being achieved. Discussion is essential, so that the rider is fully aware of what the instructor has in mind. Video can be most helpful at this stage. Riders should read *Manual No 2*, pages 183–187.

Discourage over-jumping — one good round over bigger fences is enough. Little schooling is needed during the season if the horse is going well.

These fences must never be left at full height for less experienced members to attempt.

American show hunter jumping

Training will be similar to the above, but the emphasis is even more strongly on the 'dressage' aspects of jumping. A regular, rhythmic canter stride throughout, correct leads and bend, straightness through lines of fences, are just as important as the horse's style over fences.

'Round the ring' jumping

Where this is used, it is even more important to make use of trotting poles and jumping at different paces, and to insist that the pony is steadied and 'rounded up' between fences.

HORSE TRIALS

Requirements: Courses/fences to suit the level. See below.

Reference: *Manual No 1*, pages 108–110, and *Manual No 2*, pages 73–77.

Novice riders, Introductory Trials. Before entering, members should have completed at least one junior riding test and a show-jumping event. They should have been taught at rallies to ride up and down hill and to jump small ditches, logs and natural fences. See pages 120–122.

For dressage and show jumping see foregoing pages.

Riding a cross-country course

Lesson 1. The key words to bear in mind are control, calmness and confidence. Before the lesson, work out a course of six to eight fences in a fairly small area. It could include a straightforward, two-stride double, and, if possible, about the middle of the course, a fence where the pony must be steadied back to trot. Otherwise, it should be possible to maintain a steady canter. Height about 55–70cm (1ft 10in to 2ft 4in).

Walk the course with the ride, preferably on foot, but if mounted, without showing the ponies the fences. Point out the importance of checking the going, the gradients, any over-hanging branches or other snags, and not covering any unnecessary distance, as well as the way to ride each obstacle.

During the work-in, check that everyone can control their pony and keep an even pace when cantering in the open.

Work individually over a practice fence, jumping from a long approach, keeping an even pace before and after, pulling up smoothly and walking back to the ride. Then work over the 'steadying' fence, and any others you think advisable.

Line the ride up where they can watch and comment, and have each member ride the course individually. With proper preparation, as outlined, they should all go clear, but any who have problems should ride part or all of the course again.

Discuss the special fitness required for cross-country. Ask all to read *Manual No 1*, pages 108–110, before the next rally.

Subsequent lessons. When riders are showing control and confidence over short courses, longer distances may be introduced, but still within earshot of an instructor with a loud-hailer. Use start and finish flags, and teach how to slow down gradually at the end of the round, dismount, run up stirrups and slacken girth, turn pony's head to the wind if he is blowing, walk him round. This will be the procedure on the day.

For introductory grade, the speed is 300m per minute, so there should not be time faults if the pony maintains a steady canter and the rider does not take a longer track than necessary. To prove this to riders, it is helpful to measure the course and time each one over it.

Explain rules re refusals, giving way to overtaking riders if you are in difficulty, leaving at walk if eliminated, prohibited assistance.

Also discuss the care of the pony on the day, and the importance of keeping him warm between the jumping phases.

Intermediate riders, Pre-training and Training Trials. It is especially important at this stage to check the jumping position over all types of fences. The top picture on page 57, *Manual No 2*, is an excellent model — all should study it. Check that stirrups are not too long. They should be shortened at least three holes from the length on the flat.

Heights may be gradually increased to 75–85cm (2ft 6in–2ft 10in), with spreads in proportion. Introduce more combinations, including bounces, corners, small jumps into water, ditch in front of a fence, obscure landings, bigger drops, but only on good going. Point out how much an unsteady rider disturbs the pony's balance and concentration.

Explain the principles of alternative fences, how to walk them and work out the best track for your pony. It is essential to walk all alternatives, so you can take the easy way out in case of trouble, or if a change of plan becomes necessary. *Manual No 2*, pages 76–77.

Speed increases to 350m per minute for Pre-training and 400m per minute for Training grades. Practise canter at the appropriate pace beside a vehicle and other exercises to develop judgment of speed and distance. See *Manual No 2*, pages 51–52, and page 134, *Manual No 3*.

Advanced riders, Open Trials to Championship level. These riders will get much of their cross-country practice and experience in competition, but training will still be needed, especially for any specific problems that may arise.

Jumping without reins (and stirrups, if fit enough) will further improve the strength and balance of the cross-country position. See *Manual No 2*, pages 181–182.

Cross-country type gymnastic exercises and practice over fences involving technical problems — not full size — are invaluable to keep horse and rider 'sharp'.

Finding the pony/horse's best pace across country, being able to 'set him up' for a fence, appreciating the dangers of dropping him in front of a solid fence at cross-country pace are all aspects that need constant attention on the part of the instructor.

Speed for D.C. is 455m per minute, for A.1. 485mpm. Every effort should be made to teach riders to judge their pace to within a few seconds of the time allowed. Excess speed must be discouraged, especially with ponies.

At this level, pay particular attention to fitness programmes for horse and rider. Emphasise the importance of regular steady exercise.

TETRATHLON

Requirements: A short, simple cross-country course.

Training must concentrate on frequent changes of horses, so that members will learn to sum them up and come to terms with different types as quickly as possible.

Help should be sought from other local organisations for training for other phases.

SPORTSMANSHIP

Throughout training, the emphasis should be that a 'personal best' is of greater value than a win at any price. Encourage a good spirit among members, make sure that the 'lesser lights' achieve their share of success and recognition.

Pony Club members should not enter for competitions unless they have had adequate training and, in their instructor's opinion, they and their ponies are up to the necessary standard.

9
OTHER PONY CLUB ACTIVITIES

A Pony Club trek through glorious scenery, well off the beaten track.

TREKS

Trekking is really an extension of the 'riding out' detailed on page 116. As a basis for planning, three examples of different types of treks will be given, but first, some general principles.

Personnel. It is extremely foolish to stage treks of any kind without adequate skilled personnel. In certain conditions, the entire party could be put in danger if those in charge lack knowledge and experience of the terrain and its inherent risks.

One person must be in overall charge, to be referred to for all decisions. Practical experience of this branch of riding and in dealing with people is essential, as well as organising ability, a quiet authority and a sense of humour.

All helpers must be capable riders, suitably mounted, and used to controlling children. Even for smaller groups there should be three adults to cope in emergency, unless there is a responsible older member who could go for help, preferably with a companion. For larger parties a minimum of one helper to five children will be required — more if the riders are inexperienced or the terrain difficult.

At least one helper should have a knowledge of first aid. This is a 'must' for treks going into remote areas.

Personnel should meet beforehand and discuss all aspects of the trek, so that everyone has a clear picture of the whole enterprise.

Planning. Maximum distance to be covered in one day, 32km, (20 miles) depending on the ability and fitness of riders and horses and the type of country. These factors will also govern the speed of travel — approximately 5–6km/3–4 miles per hour.

Check the route, as for taking rides out (page 116). In unknown territory, local Pony Clubs can often suggest contacts and may be able to help with overnight accommodation. While the route should be as interesting as possible, it should always be planned with the weakest member in mind.

Check on suitable places for breaks and for the lunch-time stop-over. This should be a sheltered area where ponies can be tied up. Water must be available here, or in the last kilometre (more than ½ mile) before lunch. Either permanent or temporary toilet arrangements will be needed. These, and tying rails, may have to be set up beforehand.

Notification. Notice of the proposed trek must be given in plenty of time, depending on its type and duration. Not less than a month of regular exercise will be needed if pony and rider are to be fit enough to enjoy the trek and not be a burden on others.

Application forms stating simple rules and requirements should be signed by the intending rider and by a parent or guardian. Applications should not be automatically accepted — clubs must reserve the right to refuse those they feel would be unable to keep up, to look after themselves or their ponies, or known to be a disruptive influence.

Minimum age of rider depends on the type of trek, the age-group of the majority and the number of helpers available. Most treks are unsuitable for those under ten years unless they are accompanied by an adult.

Suggested minimum age for ponies is four years for one-day treks, provided they are in good condition and not carrying a heavy rider. They should not take part in longer treks under five years.

Equipment. Successful applicants should be given a list of equipment, including:

A well-fitting saddle with numnah or folded blanket, bridle, halter and rope, binder twine for tying-up.

A hoof-pick, a small brush and towel.

A raincoat, to be tied on the saddle at all times, with leather straps or laces, not with string.

Other equipment, depending on the type of trek and the time of year, should be clearly specified.

For a one-day trek, the list should state whether lunch will be provided, or whether applicants are to bring their own.

Applicants should be told to check the fitting and soundness of all saddlery and to see that their pony is well shod. If much road work is involved, road shoes are better than concaves.

Final check. About a week beforehand, the leader should personally check:

Ponies — condition, feeding and shoeing.

Saddlery — soundness and fitting.

Riders — that they are 'riding fit'.

Before setting out. Inspect thoroughly, paying particular attention to ponies' feet, which should have been picked out.

On trek. Have experienced helpers in the lead, to set the pace, and at the rear, to pick up stragglers and generally keep an eye on things. The trek leader should be mobile, assisting where needed.

On the road. See 'Taking Rides Out', page 116. If it is absolutely necessary to ride along or cross a busy road with a large group, Ministry of Transport assistance should be arranged beforehand.

On farm land. Cantering and jumping are not suitable activities when on trek, and the pace is best kept to walk and an occasional trot. With a big group, it is essential to appoint a responsible person to see that all gates are left as found.

ONE-DAY TREKS

It is important to have a back-up vehicle with a float so that lame or over-tired ponies (or riders) can be picked up. The vehicle could also carry lunch, cold/hot drinks, feed and covers for the ponies, insect repellent, sunburn and insect bite cream and other basic first-aid requirements.

No stage should be longer than two hours, and three to four hours overall is usually ample for younger riders. If either ponies or riders show signs of tiredness, a short period of leading the ponies may help all parties.

Walk or lead the ponies the last kilometre before the lunch break, so that they arrive cool. Tie ponies up, unsaddle, brush saddle, girth and bridle marks, check for injuries, pick out feet.

Ponies should not be hot, but if they are, limit the water to a few mouthfuls until they have cooled down. It is best to let them have a short drink whenever the opportunity arises en route, rather than waiting until they are really thirsty.

Ponies must be held out so that they can have a pick of grass if no other feed is provided at the stopping place. Make sure that all riders are familiar with poisonous plants of the countryside.

During the lunch break, ponies must not be sat on or ridden about. The break should be for a minimum of one hour — more if the weather is hot. In this case, it is better to set out earlier and have a longer break.

After lunch and a rest, a game or swim for riders may help to loosen up stiff muscles.

Before continuing, check that the site is clear of all rubbish and that toilet holes are filled in. Check ponies' feet and saddlery.

At the end of the day, ensure that ponies come in cool. Remind riders that the ponies must be well brushed over and examined for injuries before being fed and turned out. Next day, they should be looked over again and trotted up to check for soundness.

This type of trek will probably be more attractive to novice and junior riders, but it is good preparation for all, before tackling more ambitious expeditions.

TREKS INVOLVING OVERNIGHT CAMPS

The route must be well planned and suitable campsites arranged beforehand. Permanent buildings such as woolsheds or shearers' quarters are especially good, since they have cooking and washing facilities laid on, while grazing and yards are usually available in the immediate vicinity.

Two vehicles accompanying the trek is the minimum requirement. One, with float, carries all daily needs, as above, plus shoeing gear, including some spare shoes, and should be in touch with the riders throughout. The second vehicle carries all camping gear — sleeping bags, blankets, personal belongings, cooking utensils and food. Also covers and feed for the ponies. Shovel, saw, hammer and nails may be needed to provide emergency toilets, clean up yards and mend broken rails, and should also be included. This vehicle proceeds direct to the next camp, so that all is ready on arrival of the trekking party.

Catering details are not included here, since catering in camp is common to many outdoor sports. As always, planning ahead is the chief ingredient for success, and there must be one person in overall charge. Parental assistance will be vital in this department, and local schools, Boy Scouts and Girl Guides and tramping clubs would all be useful sources of information and advice.

Paddocks used for grazing must be checked beforehand for safety and water supply. Usually, after a day's trekking, ponies will settle down well together in a big paddock, but a smaller one should be available where bossy or injured ponies can be kept apart.

Hard feed will nearly always be required on long treks, and this must be fed separately. Hay may be fed out in numerous small piles, not less than 3 lengths apart.

HIGH-COUNTRY TREKS

The first essential is that ponies and riders are fit enough to cope with the terrain. Two compulsory one-day treks, on rough hill country if possible, are suggested to ensure this.

If the trek leader is not personally familiar with the territory to be ridden, arrangements must be made for a guide who knows it intimately and can decide with the property owners on the exact route to be taken. He will also know how to cope with the hazards likely to be encountered. Helpers on this type of trek must have experience of dealing with such things as bogs, shifting shale and shingle, river crossings, under-runners, rough scrub and steep rocky gullies.

Sudden changes of temperature are normal in the high country, and hypothermia is a real danger to riders and ponies alike. A warm jersey and a parka must always be carried, and covers are essential for the ponies at night, even if they are not usually covered at home. The emergency first-aid kit, carried with the party at all times, must cater for the greater risk of sun and wind burn, and should include barley sugar. For ponies, there should be anti-tetanus, antihistamine and colic relief injections. It is vital to know of riders with medical conditions. *Nobody must ever become separated from the main party.*

It is helpful at lunch time or other stops, if ponies have been trained to tether to tussocks or to knee hobble.

When in camp ponies must be checked just before dark and first thing in the morning by a knowledgeable person. Look for colic symptoms, abnormal respiration (tiredness stress shows up here), prickles, filled legs.

Trekking in any form ought to be a leisurely and companionable activity. Discipline must be sufficient to ensure safety, but the atmosphere should be as relaxed as possible, consistent with this.

Older members should be encouraged to plan and organise their own expeditions, possibly as part of their work towards the Duke of Edinburgh Awards, but they should always be accompanied by an adult.

While the non-competitive nature of trekking will be one of its principal appeals for many people, it also forms an excellent basis of knowledge and experience for those who wish to compete in long-distance and endurance riding.

CAMPS

For many Pony Clubs, the annual summer camp is the highlight of the year. It can include any of the foregoing activities, particularly one-day treks, scavenger hunts and mock hunts or paper chases — the things for which it is difficult to find time at rallies. It offers wonderful opportunities for the practical teaching of care and consideration for the pony.

For full enjoyment, fitness of rider and mount is again a prerequisite, but care must be taken that the programme is not too exhausting, especially for younger children and their ponies. A midday rest is essential for all, equine and human — including the instructors!

It is impossible to give detailed programmes, as so much depends on the situation, facilities, the instructors available, number and standard of those attending, whether actually camping or attending daily.

Campsites are usually chosen for the opportunities they offer, such as beach, farm or forest rides, and it is important to ensure that each age-group gains the maximum benefit and enjoyment from whatever is available. There will probably be less jumping gear to hand than on the Pony Club ground.

It can be useful to have a theme for the instruction in each ride. For example:

Juniors. Polishing up work for D Certificate, possibly towards sitting test at the end of the week. Learning canter. Trotting over scattered poles. Riding out and about. Great care needed near water!

D–C. Improving partnership with pony — clear aids and good paces and transitions. Working on a simple dressage test or Prix Caprilli.

C–C+. How to learn new movements. Working on a simple musical or activity ride to be presented at the end of the week.

C+–B. Learning new movements and allowing time to establish with daily practice. Working out individual future programmes.

Seniors. Lateral movements. Lunging, horse and/or rider.
Rides could be asked at preceding rallies whether there is anything they would especially like to work on.

If outside instructors or lecturers are invited, be sure to make the best use of their talents or specialities.

Total daily instruction should not exceed one hour approximately for juniors to two hours for seniors, but it should be regular, to take advantage of the opportunity of several consecutive days' practice to establish anything new.

If the camp is in another club's territory, it could be good to invite them for a video or horse management quiz evening, and for an inter-club games day as a wind-up.

HUNTING

Clubs in hunting districts should work in with the local hunt club, and members encouraged to hunt when they reach the minimum age (if any) and can look after themselves without interfering with others. The pony must be under control when galloping and jumping in a crowd, and able at least to jump spars.

A course of instruction for newcomers to hunting could include the following:

Talk, well before the start of the season, on what is entailed — condition, fitness and preparation needed for pony. Read 'Hunting', *Manual 1*, pages 77–78.

Training. Jumping spars, wire, ditches and any special obstacles likely to be met locally. Opening and shutting gates. Manners of pony.

Talk on dress and turnout for hunting. Hunt livery — reasons for traditional dress. Use of hunting whip. Turnout of Pony Club members.

Invite local Master or Deputy Master to talk about the hunt — administration, hunt servants, hounds, kennels, etc., 'Cap', who and how much to pay. Finding out venues of meets. Conclude with demonstration of calls on the horn, if possible.

Farm ride — recognition of crops, stock in paddocks.

Visit to kennels to learn more about hounds.

Talk on hunting etiquette, behaviour in the field.

Mock hunt, preceded by talk on hunting terms. Older members act as Master, Deputy Master, huntsman, hounds and hare.

Talk on care of the pony on the day, from setting off to return. Other activities could include a children's hunt and attending a hound show.

10
PONY CLUB GROUNDS

Good tying rails are one of the first essentials at Pony Club grounds.

Pony Club grounds vary tremendously, from the big city clubs who own or lease property with the size and capacity to graze nearly all their members' ponies and horses, to small country clubs which have the use of grounds for rallies, but no grazing.

Whatever the circumstances, certain facilities are essential to cater for all the foregoing activities and instruction, while other facilities are highly desirable.

Among the essentials for rallies and competition days are:

Flat ground. Required for:
1. Teaching beginners.
2. Establishing paces, and training at all levels.
3. All basic jumping, and for games.
4. Parking cars and floats.
5. Running competitions.

For average-sized clubs, a minimum of two hectares (five acres) of land will be needed for these purposes. In hilly districts where flat land is hard to find, it would be worth considering the use of a bulldozer to level a reasonable working area. Consult parents — some may be able to help, or know somebody who could. There is a possibility of a grant from the local council or the Council for Recreation and Sport, or local service clubs might be prepared to contribute money and/or labour to such a project.

Continually working, or playing, on the side of a hill can be dangerous, is frustrating, and puts considerable strain on ponies.

TYING-UP RAILS

It is probably true to say that more accidents occur through poor tying-up facilities than from any other cause. Sufficient well-constructed tying rails are essential.

JUMPING EQUIPMENT

This should be safe and solid, but not too heavy to be handled by women and children. It will include:

Poles. Recommended length, 4m (13ft) (must be cut to same length), diameter approx. 10cm (4in), average, preferably round. Rustic and painted. Use good strong colours alternated with white in wide bands, or plain colours. Allow at least four of each colour.

Trotting poles may be a little shorter, but should be fairly heavy. They need not be painted.

Stands or ends. Lowest setting not more than 30cm (1ft), at least three cups per stand. Half could be 'shorties' up to 90cm (3ft). These are cheaper, lighter, take less storage space and are better for leaving out for members to use.

These are the basics — for filling and other desirable jumping material, see below.

In some districts, owing to vandalism by outsiders or misuse by members, it may be necessary to put jumps away after use. In this case, a lock-up shed will be needed. Otherwise, an open-fronted shed will protect the gear from the weather when not in use.

Sound external fences and gates. See 'Pony Club Grazing', below.

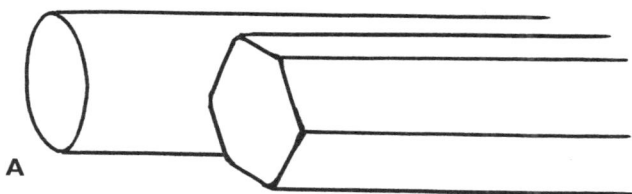

A

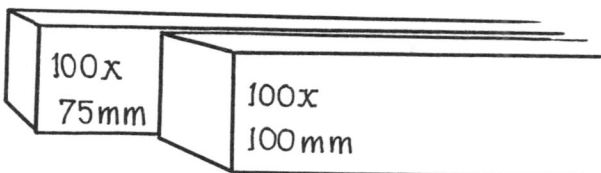

100x
75mm

100x
100mm

B

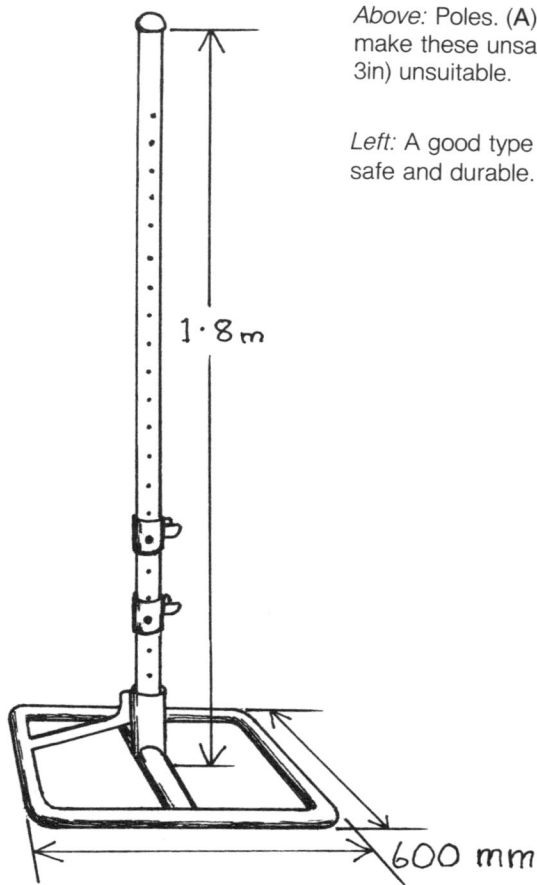

1·8 m

600 mm

Above: Poles. (**A**) Safe. (**B**) Sharp edges make these unsafe. 100 by 75mm (4in by 3in) unsuitable.

Left: A good type of jumping stand — light, safe and durable.

GAMES EQUIPMENT

Bending poles should be 1.5m (5ft) long, 15cm (6in) in ground, 2.5–5cm (1–2in) in diameter, flags, cones or other safe markers, buckets (minus handles), sacks, etc.

DRESSAGE ARENAS

Arenas may be constructed of ropes and standards, poles on the ground, picket fence, plastic piping. (For permanent arenas, see page 207.)

Ropes and standards. Rope should be lightweight, light-coloured, not blue or green, on a spool to prevent tangling. Hempen rope is usually too heavy and tends to stretch, making it difficult to keep it taut.

Standards should be approximately 60cm (2ft) in height. Corners must be reinforced, especially if rope is heavy. Electric fence standards and tape are not suitable. The standards are too high, riders' feet may easily catch on them and ponies are often afraid of the tape.

Setting up an arena

Requirements, 40 by 20m: standards, four corners, two gateway and seven plain, total 13, rope, 122m.

60 by 20m: standards, four corners, two gateway, 11 plain, total 17, rope, 162m.

Letters.

It is *essential* that the sides should be straight and the corners square, otherwise it will be impossible to work correctly in it. You will need a 20m measuring tape.

Method:
1. Measure one long side, insert corner standards. Stretch the rope on the ground round the corner standards.
2. Measure 4m on long side, X–Y, put in a peg.
3. Measure 3m on short side, X–Z, and adjust rope until measurement Y–Z equals 5m, put in a peg.
4. Retaining this line, measure 20m to next corner and insert standard. Having squared one corner, measure the next long side, and adjust the fourth corner standard until the remaining short side measures 20m.

While measuring, lay all markers where required. When the rope is raised, it will give a straight line and these standards can be put in accordingly. *Note:* The term 'quarter-marker' is misleading. They are set 6m from the corners on the long sides.

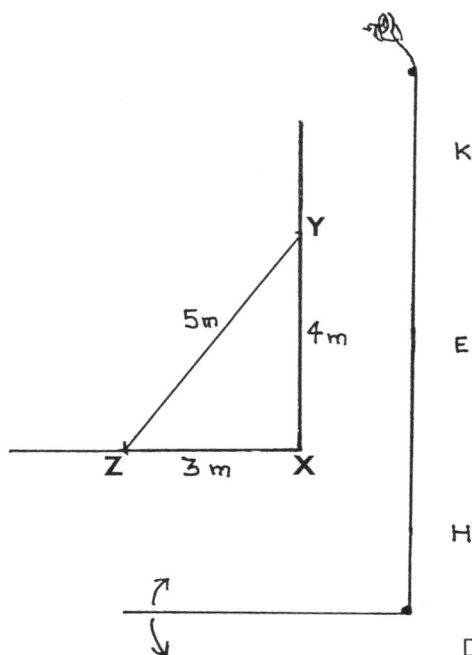

Dressage arena, squaring corners.

Dressage letters are most helpful for all teaching, and essential when working on tests. A useful aid for setting them out correctly (starting from the quarter-marker to the right of the gateway, facing in) is the phrase: 'Five Black Manx Cats Had Eleven Kittens Apiece!'

For the long arena, the extra markers are placed midway (12m) between the half and quarter markers. Starting between B and M and going anti-clockwise, they are R, S, V, P.

The letters should be placed 2m from the rope, opposite the marker.

A marked centre line is essential for competition, and very useful for training.

When poles on the ground are used, there must be two poles for each corner and one at every marker, except A, but there may be gaps between the poles along the sides. It is just as important as with ropes that the sides should be straight and the corners square. Either place the letters close up to the poles, or, preferably, use marker pegs and set the letters back, as for a roped arena.

Picket fencing, although attractive, is expensive, and difficult to erect and maintain. Plastic piping is also expensive, but very safe and maintenance-free.

CLUBROOM

As a focal point, for lectures, HQ on competition days, refuge in bad weather, for committee meetings and courses. It should have:

1. Power.
2. Telephone, for quick communication in the event of an accident and for members' use. To be reached through a hatch from the outside, and set for local calls only. Numbers of doctor, vet, farrier, etc., should be available close by the phone.
3. First-aid boxes for rider and horse. Even if there is no clubroom, these should always be available at rallies. Anything used must be replaced promptly.
4. Notice board.
5. Benches or stacking chairs, table(s) for lectures, etc.
6. Refrigerator, for cold drinks. Also useful for ice packs when needed.
7. Tea- and coffee-making facilities — water heater, sink, plastic mugs, storage space.
8. Wall charts, posters, blackboard, etc. See page 78.
9. Copies of Pony Club manuals and other 'recommended reading', for reference by both members and instructors.
10. Strong door-lock, and bars on windows.
11. Toilets — if only of a temporary nature.

Other, 'highly desirable' facilities include:

Undulating ground, essential for teaching certain aspects of cross-country riding, and there are many benefits to be gained from hill work by riders at all stages. See page 115. It could be possible to make banks and mounds which would be invaluable for training. A tractor and front-end loader can work wonders.

A measured distance, marked out by posts at 100m intervals round a large, flat or slightly undulating, paddock, is invaluable for teaching judgment of speed and distance.

Further jumping equipment. To start with, the basic poles and stands will suffice, but more variety will soon be needed.

Cavalletti. Useful for early jumping, trotting work, gymnastic exercises and activity rides. They must never be used piled up to make larger fences, or on slopes.

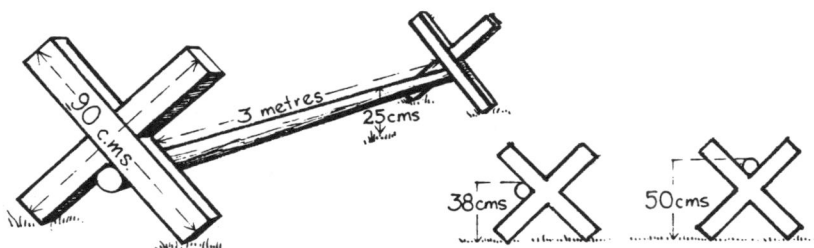

Construction details of cavalletti.

Solid obstacles — walls, brush fences, gates, etc. Always start with a miniature specimen, maximum 45cm (1ft 6in). This can be used by almost all members, and will serve as filling for bigger fences for the more advanced. Then go on to medium size, 60–75cm (2ft 6in), and finally 90cm (3ft) approximately. Remember that walls, in particular, cannot be sloped or altered, and, if too big, greatly increase the risk of over-facing.

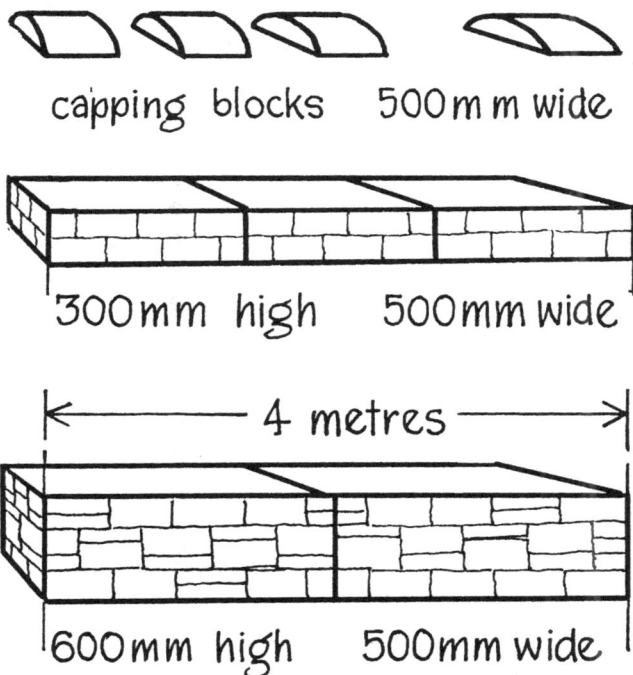

capping blocks   500mm wide

300mm high   500mm wide

|← 4 metres →|

600mm high   500mm wide

Construction of walls. Larger ones should have a broader base for stability.

201

Solid fences are best built either on skids or in two or three sections, for greater portability. In the latter case, they must fit closely together so that there are no gaps that feet could slip through.

Brush fences require a frame to be filled and freshened up as necessary.

Drums must have the ends in and be in sound condition. Different sizes are most useful. The large, 44-gallon drums should not be used standing upright.

Wire jump, preferably in two sizes. Useful in areas where 'round the ring' jumping is popular, and in hunting districts for getting ponies going over wire.

CROSS-COUNTRY FENCES

Most riders thoroughly enjoy cross-country riding, and it is unequalled for developing confidence and ability. Basically, most cross-country courses will include some open, free-going fences, jumping up and down hill, and fences on different levels, ditches and water, and combinations, often involving turns or offering alternatives. Even introductory courses are sometimes fairly technical, so both riders and ponies have to be trained to cope with the problems they may meet. Good training is only possible if suitable facilities are available for regular use.

Cross-country schooling fences are best built in small groups which can be seen from one vantage point by an instructor. Eventually fences from each group can be joined up to make one or more courses round the property, but a long course is useless for training.

If they are not adjustable, there should be different sizes of the same type of obstacle side by side. It is essential that there are small fences suitable for riders of Pre-C standard (height 45–60cm/1ft 6in–2ft) and for young ponies and horses. Trying to make a start over larger fences leads to over-facing and unnecessary stress.

The siting of fences is of paramount importance. Advice should be sought from a skilled Pony Club course designer/builder, so that the best possible use can be made of the ground and materials available. Poorly built or sited fences can be extremely dangerous.

The following suggestions have been well proven, both in training and competitive situations:

Recommended minimum dimensions of rails: length, 5m (16ft), diameter 15cm (6in).

Slip-rails are an easy way of making fences adjustable, but still solid. The fittings must be such that the rail cannot bounce in any direction.

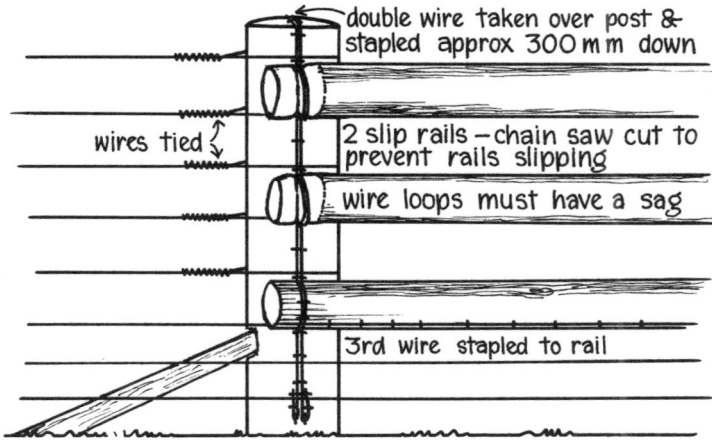

double wire taken over post &
stapled approx 300 mm down

wires tied

2 slip rails – chain saw cut to
prevent rails slipping

wire loops must have a sag

3rd wire stapled to rail

Slip-rails are useful to make cross-country fences adjustable.

Logs of different sizes always jump well and are invaluable.
Fences on slopes *must* be fixed — they are dangerous if they roll.
Special care is needed as to their type and siting.

all fences ⟶

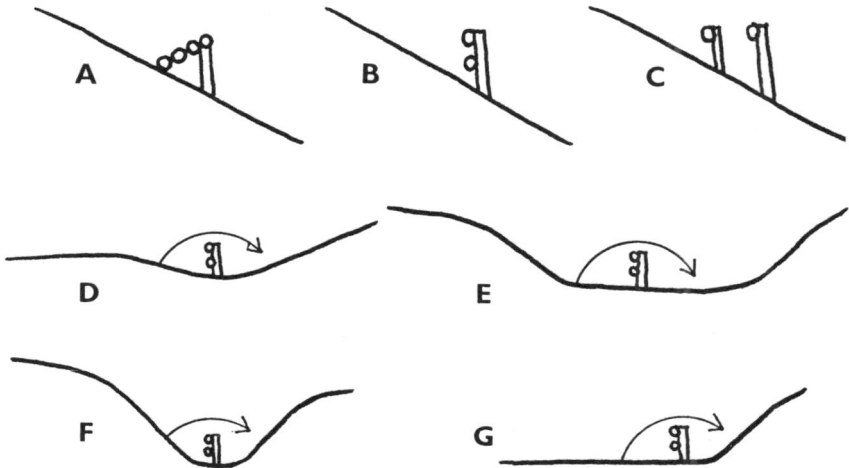

Fences on slopes. (A) Ramp. Requires controlled, bold approach, but safe.
(B) Upright post and rails — difficult, horse may slide into bottom. (C)
Parallels — dangerous, should not be used. (D) and (E) Acceptable. (F) and
(G) Both dangerous — landing into bank. Horse may overreach.

Banks. Even where there is undulating ground, banks provide end-less opportunities for training. They may be used in conjunction with show-jumping fences to form combinations and gymnastic exercises of all types. The labour involved in building a bank is well worthwhile.

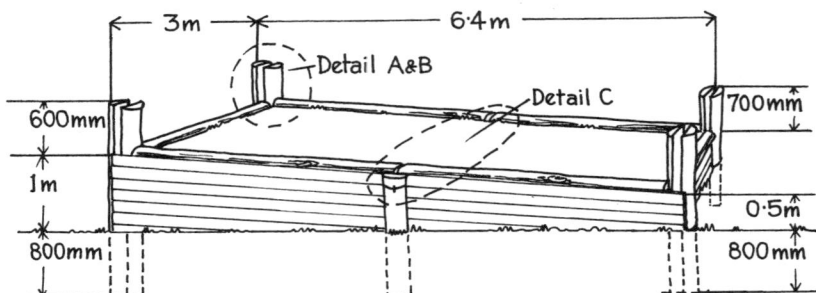

A schooling bank.

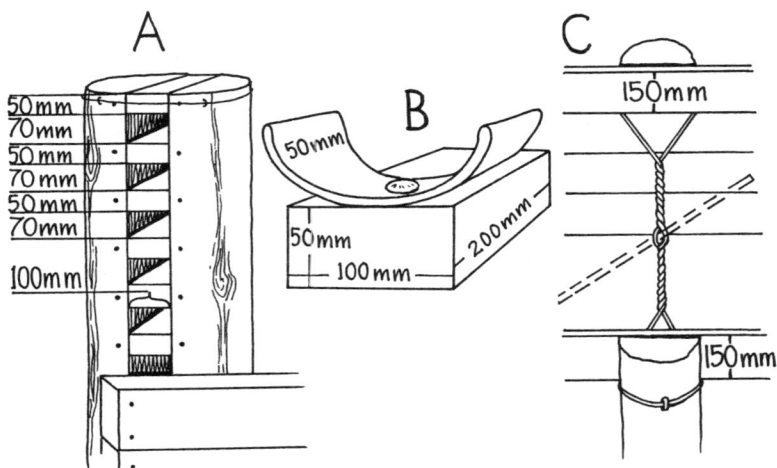

Construction details of bank.

Ditches. Most ponies have an inbuilt distrust of ditches. At least two sizes will be required for training purposes. They must be solidly faced, and the top of this facing must not have sharp edges, which could injure a pony's tendons if he slides into it. For construction details see pages 206–207.

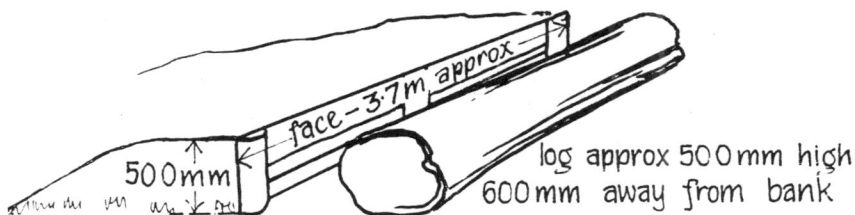

face – 3.7m approx

500mm

log approx 500mm high
600mm away from bank

Easy start 'ditch'. May be jumped from either direction.

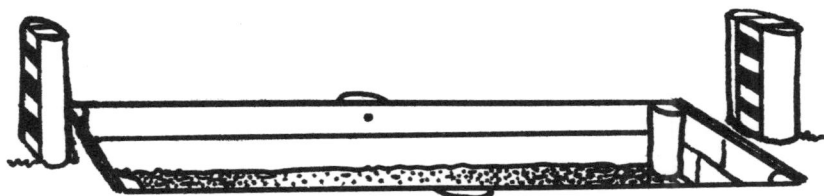

3.7m X 800mm
½ round capping rails or sleepers
1 centre upright .... blocks at the ends
otherwise same as BIG DITCH

'Baby' ditch.

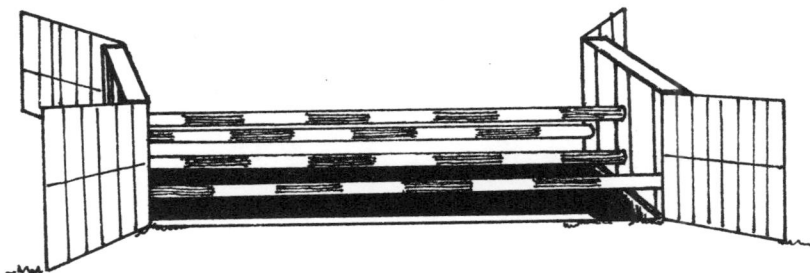

Hog's back over big ditch.

A. top view   BIG DITCH

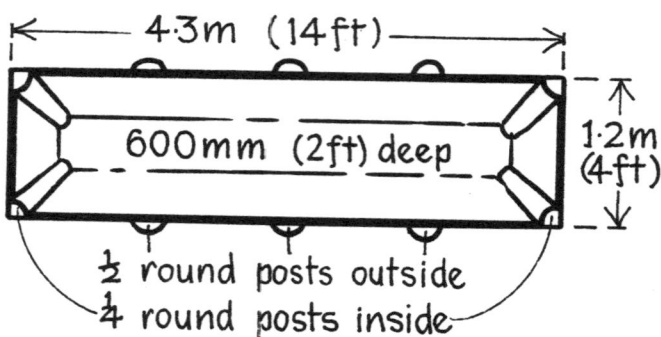

← 4·3m (14 ft) →

600mm (2ft) deep

1·2m (4ft)

½ round posts outside
¼ round posts inside

B. inside walls   BIG DITCH

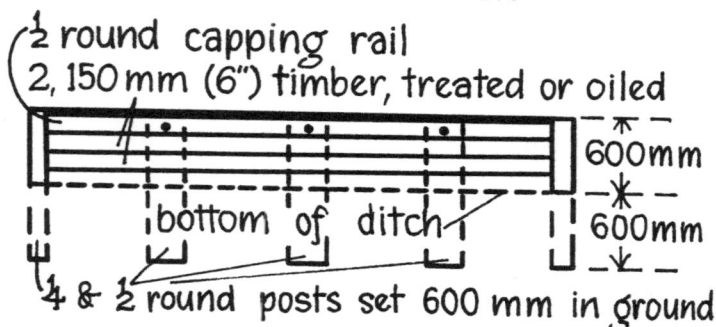

½ round capping rail
2, 150 mm (6") timber, treated or oiled

600mm

bottom of ditch

600mm

¼ & ½ round posts set 600 mm in ground

C. detail of ¼ & ½ round posts & capping rail

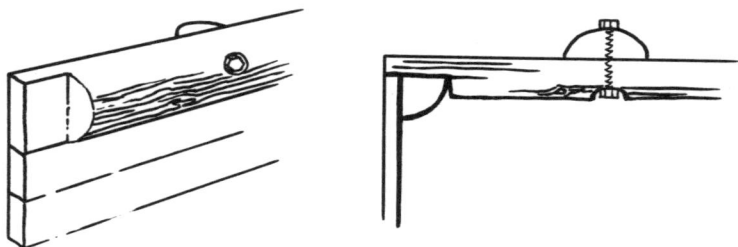

Construction details of big ditch.

D. jump supports & wings

jump supports + top & base · 150×50 mm timber.
wings · packing case or similar · oiled or creosoted
cups & blocks as for bank

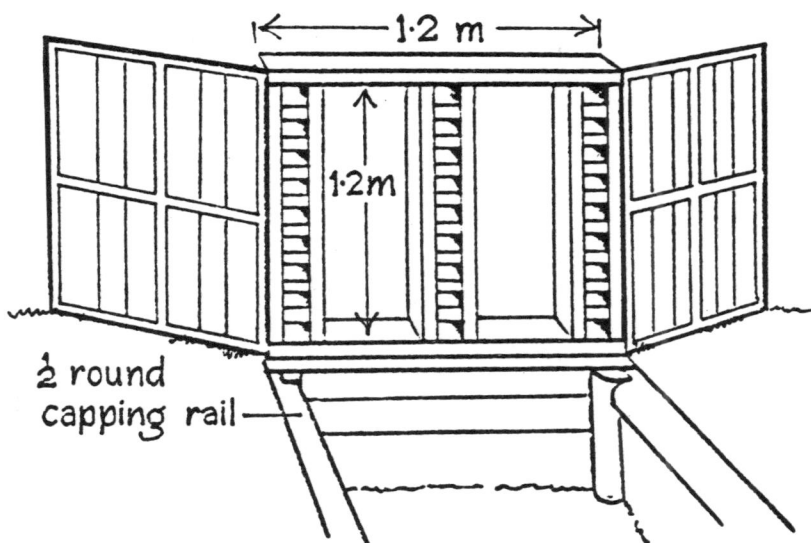

When building 'alternative' fences, all routes must be viable, but the theory that the longer routes should have easier fences than the direct track should always be borne in mind.

See also pages 136 and 208 for other cross-country fences.

Fences on skids which can be towed by a vehicle and resited, thereby setting-up fresh problems, can be very useful.

ALL-WEATHER ARENAS

Invaluable in areas where the ground becomes very hard or boggy, or where space is limited and the paddock is used for grazing. Avoids cutting up the ground and making tracks.

Dressage. Recommended size 40 by 20m.

Lunging. Minimum size, 20m square; recommended, 25m. Extremely useful where an enclosed dressage arena is not available, and the club has A and H candidates.

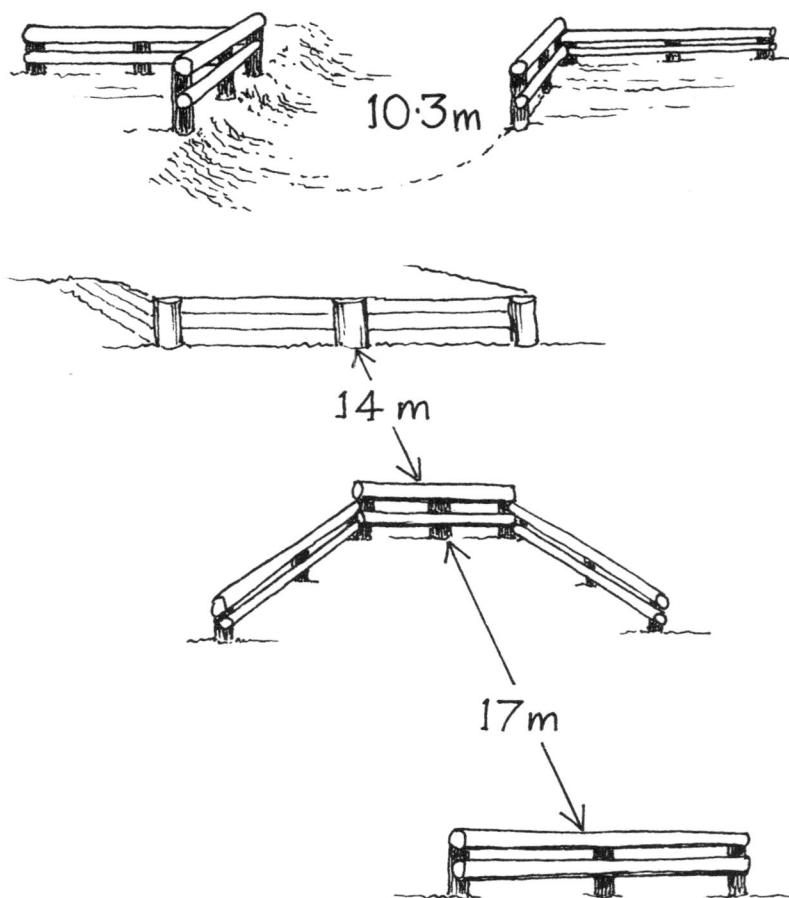

Cross-country combinations, including alternatives.

Drainage. Whatever surface is used, good drainage is the key to success. Methods vary greatly according to the locality. It will usually be necessary to remove the topsoil and to provide some form of base-course.

Surface. Depends on the soil type, and on what materials are available. It must not be too hard, either for ponies' feet, which may be unshod, or for riders in the event of a fall.

Bark or woodchips are generally best — not shavings or sawdust, which can both be dangerous in wet conditions.

Rubber chips must not be too deep, and require perfect drainage.

Dust can be a problem, and watering is of little use in very hot weather. Waste oil will keep dust down, but is very dirty and inhibits drainage.

Clubs are strongly recommended to seek advice from other clubs or individuals who have arenas, or from contractors in their area.

Any surface must be raked regularly to keep it level and to prevent compaction, and weeds must be dealt with.

Fencing. Dressage arena. Must be solid up to at least 30cm (1ft), to keep the surface material together. Should have dressage letters, which may be painted on the boards.

These arenas are generally unsuitable for competition, as people may complain that they give an unfair advantage to ponies who are accustomed to them.

Lunging arena. Minimum height 1.2m (4ft), with lower rails to prevent small ponies from escaping. Rails across the corners are useful.

TEACHING AIDS

Model jumps. Horse's skull, bones, feet. Shoes. Worms, bots. Feed samples.

A stock of bits in various sizes is a great asset, not only for lectures, but for lending to members whose ponies have bitting problems. The bits should be tried in class first.

Leather punch, and any spare items of saddlery — especially wither pads and neckstraps.

A large bell, essential at rallies, competitions, tests.

Stop-watches for competitions and for training.

Loud-hailer(s).

A public address system is expensive, but invaluable on competition days. They can be hired.

The better the facilities, the more varied, interesting and effective will the instruction be.

MANAGEMENT OF PONY CLUB GRAZING

See 'Management of a Number of Horses and Ponies at Grass', *Manual No 2*, pages 194–197.

Clubs may find it best to form a small sub-committee to manage the grounds and grazing, but there must be one person, whose authority is accepted, in overall charge of grazing arrangements.

It is recommended that paddocks be named or numbered, with the name or number on the gate. A map of the property in the clubroom, showing all paddocks and facilities, will enable newcomers to find their way around and avoid confusion.

While some paddocks will always be less popular than others, members must accept that all have to be used, and be willing to take their turn in the rotation.

Fences and gates *must* be safe and sound. Do not used barbed or high tensile wire, or cyclone netting.

Electric fences. A live wire on an existing fence stops horses leaning, and is normally safe. Some clubs are using electric fences for internal subdivision. Where it is used, both members and ponies must be carefully introduced to it and constant supervision is necessary — e.g. caretaker. It must be realised that, especially where large numbers of horses are involved, there is always a considerable risk of panic and stampede.

Water. There must be an ample, year-round supply. Large troughs in a fence-line, serving two paddocks, are excellent.

Feeding out. It is recommended that the grazing fee should include hay when required, and all horses in a paddock be fed at the same time. Hay to be in numerous scattered piles, or, if a tractor is used, in long, zigzag lines, well apart. Hay racks can lead to arguments and badly poached ground.

Hard feed is *never* to be given in the paddock among other horses. A yard, central to several paddocks, is a great asset.

HORSE HEALTH AND WELFARE

1. Although stallions may be ridden at rallies if they are well behaved, they may never be accepted for grazing at Pony Club. Neither may kickers or biters, who are likely to cause injury to people or ponies. (Kickers might be given a probationary period, with hind shoes removed, to see if they will settle down.) Most clubs

ban rigs, also extremely unpredictable, and wind-suckers and crib-biters, whose bad habits can spread rapidly through a paddockful of horses.

2. Worming. Six-weekly dosing will probably be essential, but it is best to discuss policy with the club veterinarian, and follow his or her advice as to the products to be used. It is usually advisable to stomach tube once yearly, and send random droppings for analysis after each worming. All horses must be wormed at the same time — the grazing fee could include the cost of regular medication.

New horses must be wormed on arrival, unless evidence of recent worming is produced. They must never be put straight out into a paddock with a large number of strange horses. Where possible, they should be kept in isolation for one week, to ensure freedom from infection.

3. Members must be taught to be observant, and always on the lookout for injury or illness. The following must be reported immediately:

(a) A runny nose, or a pony coughing when ridden.

(b) Swollen throat glands.

(c) Lice, ringworm or any other skin irregularities.

In all the above cases, the pony must be isolated at once.

(d) A pony off-colour — dull, mopey, off its feed.

Unless experienced assistance is immediately available, advice should always be sought on injuries or lameness.

4. Epidemics, (strangles, flu virus, etc.). Clubs should be prepared to take firm action to prevent the spread of such highly infectious diseases. New or outside ponies should not be allowed on to the grounds, and 'inmates' should not be allowed off them. Bear in mind that floats and water troughs are two of the biggest conveyers of infection. If necessary, the club should be closed.

GRAZING RULES

Clubs will of course have their own rules, but they should include provision that everybody must:

1. Obey the directions of the grazing master.
2. Attend rallies regularly.
3. Attend working bees for paddock maintenance.

ESSENTIAL FACILITIES

Tying rails. Must be solid, and binder twine provided for tying ponies.

Yards — see *Manual No 2*, pages 225–226. Clubs will find a few yards are useful for ponies that don't tie up, and for shutting up fat ponies, when necessary.

Muck heap. See *Manual No 2*, page 218.

Wash-down area with hose — invaluable for sprains, etc.

Haybarn, to enable hay to be bought when cheapest and stored. See *Manual No 2*, page 221. This is valuable even where the club does not have its own grazing, so that members may be sure of a consistent supply at a reasonable price.

An isolation paddock, for infectious cases. See *Manual No 1*, page 168. One or two small paddocks or large yards where lame or sick ponies may be cared for.

DESIRABLE FACILITIES

One or more loose boxes. For a sick horse, or where one may be held while awaiting the vet or farrier. As a teaching aid for B, A and H candidates, or for any members who may be travelling away to shows or championships. For construction, see *Manual No 2*, pages 218–220.

Larger clubs might consider:

Buying a tractor. It could serve many purposes, including:
Topping paddocks, and harrowing paddocks and dressage arena.
With a trailer, transporting jumping gear, feeding out.
With a blade and front-end loader, levelling in a small way, constructing banks and digging ditches for cross-country obstacles.
A shed will be required.

Building a forge. Encourages the farrier to attend regularly, and enables hot shoeing to be carried out. A valuable teaching aid for *all* members. Should be built under farrier's supervision.

A resident caretaker — if accommodation is available.

Provision for storage of tack, is advisable only if there is a caretaker. Individual lockers are best and safest. There should be space for cleaning tack, with saddle horses and bridle hooks, and water laid on.

MAINTENANCE

This is one of the biggest problems with Pony Club grounds. While things are new they look fine, but with constant use and the inevitable breakages and wear and tear, good maintenance is essential. Broken rails and peeling paint do nothing to encourage a sense of pride in one's club.

It should be a rule that any damage to fences, gates, tying rails, yards or jumps should be reported immediately (without fear of reprisal). A maintenance team should be appointed to deal with all such matters.

From time to time working bees will be necessary for painting, pulling ragwort, cleaning paddocks and other chores. All parents and riders must be prepared to help in a practical way when called upon by the committee.

All members must play their part in keeping the place tidy. See 'Tidiness', *Manual No 2*, page 197. Rubbish bins must be provided — and used. Older members could be responsible for the clubroom and surrounding area. The more people are involved, the greater the club spirit.

It should be emphasised that every Pony Club ground is a show-case for the club and the movement as a whole.

CONCLUSION

Pony Club is a complex system in its responsibility, administration and instruction. As mentioned on page 1 of the Introduction, we are aware that this book could appear intimidating to the newcomer wondering whether or not instructing is for them.

Just as riders develop personal goals to gain successive certificates or to compete at the highest levels, so it can be for instructors. Their aims could be to work up to Chief Instructor status, or to travel overseas and gain the professional qualifications available there.

But for every instructor with these aspirations, there are probably a hundred who are completely happy just going to Pony Club, teaching at their chosen level and thereby playing an invaluable role. Many instructors find tremendous satisfaction in working with the group often called the 'littlies'. This is perhaps the most important stage of all — it's where it all starts and where riders are taught the basics, so essential for progress later on.

One of the many strengths of Pony Club is the variety of people who become involved, all with one aim — to help children to enjoy a pastime which is renowned for developing character and initiative. So whatever your hopes (or doubts!) we trust that this book will help you to enjoy the satisfactions of instructing at Pony Club.

May your rides always be full (a sure sign of a successful instructor), and may your hopes for your riders' futures be fulfilled. Be sure that whether you teach D's or A's, you, the instructor, are an integral part of an elite, world-wide group, The Pony Club.

READING

New Zealand Pony Clubs Association *Manual No 1* and *Manual No 2*.
Also:
All the books listed in *Manual No 2*, page 301.
British Horse Society, *Instructors' Handbook*, produced for the BHS by Threshold Books Ltd. 1985.
British Horse Society, *Mounted Games and Gymkhanas*.
British Horse Society, *Ride and Drive Safely*.
Ministry of Transport, *Road Code*.
Molly Sivewright, FIH, FBHS. *Thinking Riding*, two volumes, J. A. Allen & Co.
Alois Podhajsky, *The Riding Teacher*, Harrap, London. 1973.
Pam Roberts, *Teaching the Child Rider*, J. A. Allen & Co. 1973.
John Anthony Davies. *The Reins of Life*, J. A. Allen & Co. 1987.
    Excellent for those helping with Riding for the Disabled.

NZPCA publications, available from the Association secretary:
Rules and Guidelines for Pony Club Certificates.
Pony Club Mounted Games.
Guidelines for Junior Horse Trials.
Current dressage tests and rulebooks for Teams Dressage and Horse Trials Championships.
NZPCA Instructors' Training Programme. For information contact your local Pony Club secretary.